Unions
and Change
Since 1945

Chris Baker and Peter Caldwell have
worked together for five years in trade
union education in the West Midlands.
Chris Baker worked as a Workers'
Educational Association tutor/organizer
in South Staffordshire and Shropshire
until 1978, since then he has been a
social policy analyst with a new town
development corporation. He is a
member of NALGO and lives in Telford
with his wife and two children. Peter
Caldwell works for the WEA in
Coventry teaching and organizing trade
union studies. He co-edits *Trade Union
Studies Journal* and has written on health
and safety. He is an active member of
ASTMS and lives in Leamington with
his wife and two children.

Pan Trade Union Studies

Also available in this series

C. Aldred:
Women at Work

P. Burns and M. Doyle:
Democracy at Work

A. Campbell and J. McIlroy:
Getting Organized

D. Eva and R. Oswald:
Health and Safety at Work

Series editors

Peter Caldwell
Tutor/Organizer
Workers' Educational Association
West Midlands

Alan Campbell
Lecturer in Industrial Relations
University of Liverpool

Mel Doyle
Assistant Secretary
Workers' Educational Association

Pan
Trade Union
Studies

Unions and Change Since 1945

Chris Baker and Peter Caldwell

Pan Original

Pan Books   London and Sydney

First published 1981 by Pan Books Ltd,
Cavaye Place, London SW10 9PG
© Chris Baker, Peter Caldwell and the Workers'
Educational Assocation 1981
ISBN 0 330 26475 3
Phototypeset by Input Typesetting Ltd, London SW19 8DR
Printed in Great Britain by
Richard Clay (The Chaucer Press) Ltd, Bungay, Suffolk

About the series

This series of books has been written for several groups of people – those thinking of joining a union, or new members; those who are just becoming active members; new and less experienced shop-stewards; and indeed anyone interested in trade unions today. It aims to provide an introduction to the principles of basic trade unionism by discussing a wide range of arguments and issues in the five key areas covered by the books. In straightforward language each book points the way towards the action that must be taken by individual trade unionists, and by the movement as a whole, if their goals are to be achieved.

About this book

We have written this book as trade unionists about our fellow trade unionists. We have used the aims and objectives of ordinary union members to look at the changes that have taken place in our unions since 1945. It is, therefore, very selective, in that we cannot condense the breadth of workers' experience in the past thirty-five years into one short volume. We have tried to point to what we consider to be the important changes that have taken place in union membership, organization and participation in industrial and political activity. These changes are then examined in the light of issues that are of concern to all of us: our living standards, jobs and safety. We hope that you will want to compare your own experience with those we have discussed in this book. If there are differences or similarities then why not discuss them with your colleagues at work or in your union branch? It is these discussions, and many others like them, that will determine the way unions cope with change in the next thirty years.

Acknowledgements

In writing this book we've drawn on many people's ideas. Written sources are generally acknowledged in the text. Much benefit has been gained from discussions in our own unions, in WEA industrial branches, in health and safety groups and on trade union education courses. The following people read the manuscript at various stages and made valuable comments: Cliff Allum, Gwenda Baker, Susan Caldwell, Tom Davies, Dave Eva, Chloe Gerhardt, Paul Gerhardt, Chris Ham, Sylvia Hitchins, Tony Hitchins, Stephen Wellings. We would like to thank Joan Tilby and Sue Howe who did a splendid job typing the manuscript.

To keep the book short, and hopefully readable, has meant making choices about what should be put in and what left out. The choices, and the responsibility for the final product are, of course, ours. We would like to dedicate the book to our families: Gwenda, Steffan, Rhian and Iwan, Sue, Michael and Steven.

Contents

Introduction

Can you remember a time when unions weren't strong, well organized, with a growing membership? If you can't then perhaps you are one of the five million people who have joined the labour movement since 1945. On the other hand, you might be a branch secretary of forty years standing, whose union membership stretches back further than you care to remember. You could be a miner, local government officer, a clerical worker, an engineering foreman or maybe a student or shop worker. Whatever your job, your experience of unions will certainly depend on when and where you first decided to become a member. Whether you joined an existing union set-up, or helped to establish a new union branch at your workplace, you will have played some part, however small, in changing unions and the way unions are viewed.

For those of us active in the unions, there is seldom time to stop and think about the past, and even less time to discuss it with our friends and colleagues at work. Yet past experience offers us important lessons for today and tomorrow. It helps explain how and why unions have changed and are changing in response to different pressures. This book focusses on the changes that have taken place since 1945. It is not about history as such, but about certain key themes and events which are of concern to all of us. In describing what has happened, we've had to be selective. You can perhaps think of many more examples from your own reading and experience to replace the ones we've given.

This book is in three parts. In the first part, Chapters one to three, we concentrate on change in the unions themselves. We look at three main areas: membership, workplace organization and political influence. In the second part, Chapters four to six, we look at how unions have tried to create change. We look at the role of unions in protecting workers' living standards, jobs and safety. In the final part, Chapter seven, we draw together the changes made in and by the unions as a way of helping us understand what is happening in the eighties.

Throughout the book the emphasis is on asking questions rather than supplying answers. Hopefully reading it will encourage you to look again at your own experience as well as that of your fellow trade unionists.

Chapter **One**

Who are union members?

Today, just under twelve million workers are members of trade unions. People doing all sorts of different jobs, in different industries and workplaces. In fact over half of the working population are trade union members, quite a high proportion compared with most other countries. Over the last thirty years there have been significant changes in the composition of trade union membership. The typical trade unionist, if such a person exists, is now just as likely to be a young woman working in an office or a married woman working part time in the local hospital, as to be a miner, steel worker or engineer.

In this chapter we shall be looking at:

● in which jobs union membership is high and in which it is low;

13

- how the proportion of workers who are members of unions has changed in the post war years;
- in which areas unions will need to expand their membership.

Union membership

Who are union members?

The proportion of workers who are union members varies considerably from industry to industry. This depends partly on the attitude of the employer towards recognizing the union. Generally speaking, for example, the state as an employer has taken a positive attitude towards union membership. If we look, therefore, at industries where the state is the employer, union membership is often high. In nationalized industries like the gas, electricity and water boards, British Rail or the mining industry, union membership is at least 85 per cent and often as high as 95 per cent. Similarly, employees of central government, civil servants, are very likely to be union members.

Moving to people who work for private firms in manufacturing industry, the size of the workplace is important. Research undertaken for the Government Commission into Industrial Democracy (the Bullock Report), showed that average union membership in larger workplaces, where over 200 people worked, was nearly 72 per cent. If all manufacturing workplaces were included however, the figure dropped to just over 60 per cent. In larger workplaces workers are perhaps more aware of their need to join together, and their employer more willing to accept this and talk to them through their representatives.

Where are unions weak?

On the other hand some groups of workers have found it very difficult to build up collective union organization. Here are some examples:

14

- workers who are often changing their workplaces as a particular job is completed, for example building workers;
- people who often work in small groups of twos and threes like farm workers;
- part-time workers who are frequently isolated from their full-time colleagues, a weakness which management has often been quick to exploit;
- people who work on their own at home and find it very hard to make any contact at all with others doing similar jobs;
- unemployed workers who often drop out of unions when they lose their jobs and soon lose contact with their former workmates.

Many of these people need unions as much as those working in big established workplaces. However, it is often much harder for them to build up a permanent organization.

Changes in union membership

How has union membership changed?

Another way of looking at union membership is to see how it has changed over time. We've already seen how the proportion of union members varies from industry to industry and from job to job. A term used to describe the proportion of the work-force who are union members is union density. If a large proportion of workers are members, then density is high. If only a small proportion, density is low. The graph in Figure 1 shows how union density across the whole working population has changed over the years.

The first part shows a steady increase in density from a low point in the early thirties to a peak of just over 45 per cent after the war. It took until the mid-sixties before union density moved above that level. Look again at the graph and the increase that has taken place since 1965. By 1977 nearly 53 per cent of the work-force were union members.

In the twenties the unions took a terrible battering as the employers, faced with declining markets for their goods,

15

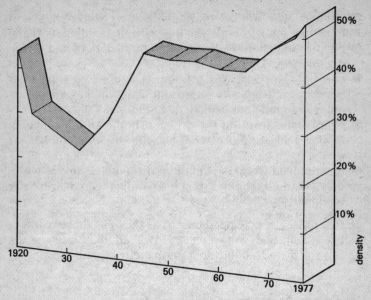

G. S. Bain and R. Price *Profiles of Union Growth: a comparative statistical portrait of eight countries*

Figure 1   Union density 1920–77

tried to claw back some of the gains that unions had made during and just after the First World War. The miners struck for nine months after the defeat of the General Strike, trying heroically to stave off cuts in wages and conditions. Earlier the engineers had been locked out for thirteen weeks as the employers attempted to increase their control over the work-force, and other sections of the movement, like the dockers, railwaymen and textile workers, faced similar attacks. By the beginning of the thirties, rock-bottom morale, mass unemployment and the real fear of victimization led to hundreds of thousands of workers leaving the unions. In 1933, there were three million less union members than in 1920.

By the mid-thirties, however, the economy had begun to pick up as Britain re-armed. Slowly, in areas like the aircraft and armament industries there was a rebirth of workers' confidence and willingness to organize. Trades councils in some areas spearheaded recruitment drives that brought hundreds of thousands of new members into the unions.

The position of the unions was completely changed by the war. Unemployment disappeared as the government conscripted workers into the forces and factories. The success of this task depended on the cooperation of the trade unions to meet the demands of the war effort. Ernest Bevin, the general secretary of the TGWU was made Minister of Labour and his Essential Work Order in 1941 made it illegal to sack a worker in an essential industry without the permission of a Ministry of Labour official. In any case, 'you can't sack a worker if you can't replace him'. Strikes were made illegal but despite this the number of strikes rose and few prosecutions took place. The government needed production. The employers needed all the workers they could get. To ensure this, the unions were brought in from the cold. In the factories, stewards were recognized and joint production committees set up. Nationally trade union officials were coopted on to government committees. With much of the fear caused by unemployment removed, the war workers flocked into the unions.

For many people, the war was a victory for collective organization at work and throughout society. A belief in this, along with a determination never to return to the thirties, underlay Labour's dramatic election victory in 1945. Strong unions were very much a part of this movement.

After the war: changing fortunes of the old guard

The years from 1945 to the end of the sixties are often presented as a period in which trade union power was consolidated. Looking at union membership though, this does not seem to have been entirely true. Union density reached a peak in 1948 and actually tailed off slightly during the fifties. Union membership was slowly growing but it was not keeping pace with the growth in the size of the work-force.

To see why this slightly surprising trend was taking place at a time of full employment and rising living standards, we need to look more carefully at how the work-force itself was

17

changing. The overall increase of its size concealed decline in some areas and growth in others. From 1948 to 1974, jobs in some industries were disappearing quickly. Figure 2 shows those where substantial job losses occurred.

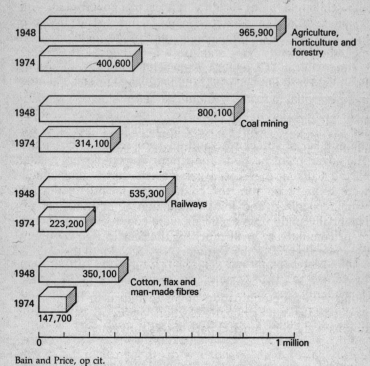

Bain and Price, op cit.

Figure 2   Job loss in selected industries 1948–74

Taken together, over 1,700,000 lost jobs. Significantly, with the exception of agricultural workers, these were all areas where trade union membership was substantial. In 1948, mining, cotton and railways had been strong and influential centres of trade unionism. The National Union of Miners, with well over 600,000 members and the National Union of Railwaymen, with nearly 450,000 members, were two of the six largest unions. They were not a great deal smaller than the largest union at that time, the Transport and General

18

Workers' Union with just over 1,100,000 members. But with all their members in the one industry, the miners and rail-waymen's unions declined with their industry.

This rapid movement of people between industries and jobs was often damaging for the people concerned. Will Paynter was one of the miners' leaders during the period of rapid run-down which really began in 1958.

'In the mining industry, after a decade of relative prosperity when coal was king in the energy empire . . . the scene changed back again to one we were more accustomed to, a crisis of over-produc-tion. The oil industry . . . became its main competitor with fuel oil. . . . It was the beginning of a programme of pit closures and manpower rundown that in a decade halved the size of the industry and the number of pits and men employed, leaving mining villages derelict.'

Will Paynter *My Generation* (Allen & Unwin, 1972)

In the early nineteen fifties there were a thousand pits. Each had a community built around them. Half these pits and communities as far apart as South Wales, Northumberland and Scotland were broken up.

The loss for the miners was clear. But it went further than the miners and their families. For, with their long traditions of solidarity and collective determination, the miners had played a crucial part in the development of the whole trade union movement. Their struggles, and often their leaders, had dominated working class history in the first half of the century. They had provided a depth of commitment, re-sourcefulness and intelligence that organized workers else-where could ill afford to see weakened.

New jobs, new members?

The loss of jobs on the railways, in the pits, on the land and in the cotton factories was accompanied by an expansion of other kinds of jobs. Where were they? Figure 3 shows areas where employment opportunities expanded rapidly.

An additional two and a half million jobs were created. These were, however, very different jobs from the ones that

19

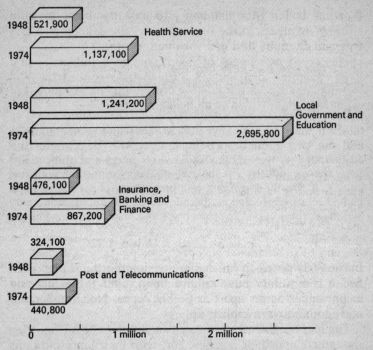

Figure 3 Job gains in selected industries 1948–1974
Bain and Price, op. cit.

were lost in traditional industries; nurses, porters, and cleaners in hospitals rather than engine drivers, signalmen and station porters. Demand for teachers and school meals workers replaced that for miners. The spinners and weavers in the cotton industry – men and women working with their hands – gave way to the huge office complexes, where nearly all the workers – filing clerks, typists, receptionists, accounts clerks, salespersons – were described as 'white collar'.

A number of important changes were working their way through the structure of the work-force:

● jobs in services, such as education and health, banking and insurance, or entertainment and catering were replacing jobs in manufacturing, extraction and certain kinds of service such as public transport;

20

- 'white collar' (non-manual) jobs took the place of 'blue collar' (manual) jobs;
- gradually more and more women went out to work.

These changes had very important implications for the sort of trade union movement that was developing at that time.

Since their foundation, the unions were predominantly male and manual. The giant unions that dominated the TUC fell into this category: the miners, railwaymen, electricians and the two general workers unions, the TGWU and the GMWU. Even the public employees' union and the clerical workers' union had a majority of male members. Yet we've seen how the traditional areas of union strength, the male and manual sectors, were losing jobs. The growth in employment was taking place in the office and in the service sector and here the trade union movement was weak. Until the end of the sixties it was not growing quickly enough in the new areas to make up for the loss in the old. It was feared that unless this was reversed unions would quickly lose their influence and become the representatives of a declining industrial minority.

White collar unions take off

Given the growth in their potential membership, the expansion of white collar trade unionism was very slow for a long time. Table 1 shows the main white collar unions with members in manufacturing industry:

Table 1 Membership of main white collar unions (manufacturing) 1948–68

Union		1948	1958	1968
draughtsmen (AESD, then DATA, then AUEW(TASS))		45,000	63,000	76,000
clerks (CAWU, then APEX)		38,000	51,000	86,000
foremen/supervisors (ASSET)	became	15,000	21,000	
scientific workers, mainly lab	ASTMS			101,000
technicians (AScW)		15,000	12,000	

TUC, *Annual Reports*

21

These figures represented a fraction of what was possible. But at least they were a start. In much of the newer private service sector, for example the insurance industry, genuine trade unionism remained relatively unknown. At that time the main strengths of white collar unionism lay elsewhere: in government employment and nationalized industries.

Towards the end of the nineteen sixties, however, this picture of relatively slow growth changed. White collar unionism began to grow quickly. A useful way of illustrating this is to look at the arrival of one of the largest and most prominent white collar unions – ASTMS.

In 1968 two unions merged to form the Association of Scientific, Technical and Managerial Staffs. One, ASSET, mainly consisted of foremen and supervisors in the engineering industry. Laboratory technicians in manufacturing industry, hospitals and universities formed the vast majority of members of the other – the AScW. Their combined membership at the time was around eighty thousand. Previously they had grown in areas where they already had members. The merger was to be the signal for an explosion in membership. This took place both within these existing areas, particularly the engineering industry, and also in a whole host of 'green field' areas like insurance and petrochemicals. The leaders of ASTMS aimed to make it a mass union of white collar workers in the same way that the general workers' unions had organized across industries and services. Their message tried to point out why white collar workers needed collective organization. This extract from a recruitment leaflet issued in 1970 is an example:

- Proper recognition of the great contribution made to the community by scientists and technicians, supervisors and management staffs.
- *A big effort to improve remuneration of those who carry responsibility, acquire skills and gain qualifications.*
- A special effort to allocate the special needs and defend the interests of those affected by the large scale mergers taking place and about to take place.
- A voice for our members in the decisions being taken which affect their work and concerns.

The attempt to get this message across to the millions of potential members was not always popular. Addressing a packed meeting of ICI supervisors in 1970, Clive Jenkins (ASTMS's general secretary) began, 'We're here to stir things up,' and went on to forecast a wages explosion in the seventies. The lesson: white collar workers had to be in there fighting. Other trade unionists were not always pleased with ASTMS's attempts to put forward the specific grievances of their potential members. Accusations of elitism were made – the term 'the elite of white collar workers' still appears on the union's membership cards. During 1970 ASTMS added another 110,000 members, nearly doubling its size. Where did they come from?

- Nearly 40,000 were engineers, some drawn from firms where the union already negotiated, others representing recognition from firms like Ford and Vauxhall who had long resisted the unionization of their 'staff';
- 10,000 new members worked in the chemical industry;
- 35,000 came from further mergers, mainly with staff associations in the insurance industry as well as direct recruitment there and in finance. A campaign in the City had been run, headed: 'My first mistake was to pick up a pen rather than a shovel.'
- The union continued to grow in the universities and health service.

The growth of ASTMS was only one sign of a white collar revolt that was taking place. They exploited it skilfully to build the union but the other white collar unions grew as well. Draughtsmen in shipbuilding and engineering had a history of union membership. Their union opened its doors to all staff in the engineering industry and grew considerably. The old clerks' union became APEX. They not only aimed for staff in engineering, but also reached out into new areas like the insurance industry. The unions we looked at in Table 1 all grew much more in the ten years after 1968 than they had in the twenty years before.

Growing pressures

Why this sudden spurt? The very fact that the number of white collar workers was growing suggests a reason for the acceleration of unionization. Offices became larger, work more repetitive and supervision more intrusive. Increasingly, techniques which had been used on the factory floor for years, like work measurement, were introduced into the office. Many of the pressures that had always encouraged manual workers to act collectively were now making themselves felt on the people working behind desks.

Redundancy is an example of this pressure. As many of the large firms merged, they were quick to begin 'rationalizing' their operations. An ASTMS officer in Manchester commented wrily that the union's best recruiting agent was Arnold Weinstock the director of the giant electrical firm GEC. The steady flow of redundancies, thirty a day since the merger with AEI and English Electric, was forcing people into the union. The seven hundred members in the GEC branch in Manchester doubled in no time at all.

The real squeeze was on pay. These were the years of strict government pay policy and this policy was not always even in its effect. Many staff workers felt they were caught in the middle. Some shop-floor workers, with their years of traditions of local, informal bargaining, were able to get round the limits by unpublicized bargains or suspect productivity deals. Senior management got in perks what they were denied in salary increases. Most office workers, negotiating a single increase annually and lacking a history of industrial muscle, saw themselves as the real losers.

Certainly there was a growing willingness to use the methods of trade union militancy in response to pressures on living standards and rising inflation. In 1964, there were only nineteen 'staff strikes' recorded in the engineering industry. In 1967 there were sixty-seven, then 130 in 1970 and 133 in 1973. At the same time inflation was rising steadily from an annual rate of 4.5 per cent in 1964 to one of 12 per cent in 1973.

We've picked out white collar workers in manufacturing

industry as an example of change in union membership and activity. They were not, of course, the only ones. An interesting parallel can be found by looking at workers in the public sector. Like white collar workers in industry, their numbers expanded rapidly. They, too, were particularly vulnerable to government pay policy, in their case because the government was their employer. The rise in their militancy was a significant feature of the 1968–74 period. This really began with the famous 'dirty jobs' strike in 1969 when dustmen stuck out for £2.50 and the rubbish piled high in the streets. Here again the rise in activity was accompanied by a dramatic increase in trade union membership. We will look in more detail at the significance of the development of public sector trade unionism in the next chapter.

Expansion in the future

A different trade union movement?

Judging by membership figures, the trade union movement has certainly radically changed over the last thirty or forty years. Many of the largest and most influential unions are now in the areas of white collar and public sector employment. The power of some of the traditionally strong unions has been eroded by their loss of membership.

Running quickly through these developments, however, a question presents itself. At one time it did look as though the unions might fail to come to terms with the changes taking place around them, that they might allow huge areas of employment to open up outside of their influence. We have seen how that was avoided in the past, but can it be avoided in the future? Similar and new trends are still working their way through the structure of work in Britain. How do you think unions will respond to them?

Let us have a look at the engineering industry as a case in point. This is the very core of manufacturing industry. Large numbers of people earn their living from it. The graph in Figure 4 shows how, when mining, cotton, railways and agriculture were declining as sources of jobs, up to the late sixties, engineering held steady, in fact it expanded modestly. Since 1970, however, this has begun to change. Slowly, employment in engineering has been declining. What the graph goes on to show is even more worrying, a projection of what employment in engineering could look like over the next twenty-five years.

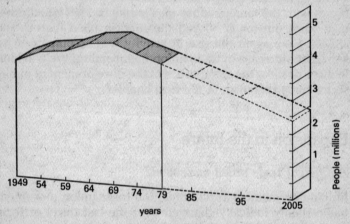

Figure 4   Future employment in engineering.
Clive Jenkins and Barrie Sherman, *The Collapse of Work* (Eyre Methuen) and Bain and Price, op. cit.

If anything on this scale does happen, and as many as one and a half million jobs are lost, what effect will it have on British workers and their unions? Will areas dependent on engineering, like the West Midlands, end up like those that were dependent on coal, like parts of South Wales?

The other related question takes us back to the beginning of the chapter when we looked at areas where unions today are weak: small workplaces, areas with a high turnover, homeworkers and part-time workers and, above all, unemployed workers. How successful will unions be in assisting these people to organize themselves? These are some of the themes we will examine elsewhere in the book but now we will turn from looking at membership strength to discuss the changing and different ways union members actually organize at their places of work.

Key points

- Workers in the public sector are now more likely to be union members than workers in the private sector.
- Certain types of work situations, where workers are divided by time and distance and lack contact with each other, have been difficult to organize.
- Up until the mid-1960s the growth in union membership barely kept pace with increases in the work-force.
- Between 1948 and 1974, 1.7 million jobs were lost in four basic industries and 2.5 million jobs were created in major public and private services. .
- The change in the industrial structure was reflected in the trade union movement. Recruitment in the new growth industries brought women and white collar workers into membership.
- The growth of unions like ASTMS illustrated the determination of white collar workers to protect jobs and living standards through collective action.
- This pattern of union membership is likely to continue to change as employment in other basic industries, like engineering, declines.

Discussion

- When and why did you join a union?
- How and when was the union first organized at your workplace?
- What changes can you foresee taking place in union membership in the future?

Further reading

It might be a good idea to start by looking for a history of your own union. Many unions, such as the Transport Workers, the Post Office Engineers and the Health Service Employees, have published readable accounts. Write to your head office for details.

Some of the themes addressed in this chapter are explored further in two books by Clive Jenkins and Barrie Sherman. They are *White-Collar Unionism* and *The Collapse of Work* (Eyre Methuen).

An interesting pamphlet on some of the problems of one particular group of workers, part-time workers, has been produced by the National Council for Civil Liberties. It's called, *Part-Time Workers need Full-Time Rights* from NCCL 186 Kings Cross Road, London WC1X 9DE.

Finally, another book in this series, *Getting organized*, talks about the 'nuts and bolts' of workplace organization.

Chapter **Two**

Representation at work: how has it changed?

For most of us, our only contact with the union is through our representative at work. Usually, in industry, that representative will be called a shop-steward, sometimes a staff, grade or departmental representative. Some industries have their own special term such as the expression 'father/mother of the chapel' which is used in the printing industry. Most places where a union is recognized will have someone responsible for taking up the problems of union members on a day to day basis. That person is one of over three hundred thousand people who form the first line of defence against management and the main link between groups of union members and the movement as a whole.

In some industries, widespread workplace representation is quite new. Many union members managed for years without it. This chapter will outline:

● the growth of workplace trade unionism in one of its traditional homes, the engineering industry;
● the different ways that employers, unions and government have reacted to the growth of workplace trade unionism;
● the ways in which groups of trade unionists have adapted the shop-steward system to suit their own particular needs;
● we will end by asking some questions about the ability of the trade union movement to continue to change so as to express the interests of its women members.

Workplace trade unionism

National and local bargaining

If you've always been used to having a steward you will probably be asking: how can you have unions without stewards? Although unions were less effective without stewards they did survive because most agreements with employers were national in scope. Wages and major conditions, like holidays, hours of work and overtime payments, would be agreed nationally between representatives of the different employers and full-time officers of the unions with members in the industry. Few issues would be taken up at the workplace although there were discussions on matters like discipline or the allocation of overtime, as well as the application and interpretation of national agreements.

There are still some industries like this. Agricultural workers are an example. Their union is recognized nationally by the farmers but is rarely recognized locally by individual farmers. This reliance on national bargaining in most industries had grown up at a time when the unions were under attack and members in the workplace faced many difficulties in getting organized. National agreements did provide some minimum standards. With full employment the unions' strength began to return, so the balance between national and local bargaining began to shift. In many industries workers found they could get much more out of their employers at a local level than they could through negotiations with all employers in that industry.

Work-group power in engineering

'Engineering' is a massive industry involving everything that is made out of metal, from paper clips to cars, lorries and aircraft. As we saw in the graph on page 26, between three and a half and four million people have earned their living in the industry since 1945. It is a stronghold of trade unionism and today one in four trade unionists is an engineering worker.

Trade union organization at the workplace has always been important as we can see if we look at the sort of work that is done and the way it is organized.

● Work is often organized on a group basis, with metal components being moved from one section to another, each section completing another stage in the process of its manufacture. The collective and interdependent nature of the work has helped to encourage a greater degree of group identity and solidarity.

● Conditions in the workplace are constantly changing. The tooling on the machine is altered for a different job, its speed changed to produce more or less. Breakdowns or shortages of components have to be coped with. A change in the job may require a different payment or number of people working on the section. All these changes created a steady flow of issues requiring negotiation between management and workers.

● Most machine workers have traditionally been paid on a piece-work basis and any change in pay involved the

31

agreement of a price for the new job. In the depths of the depression these would be given to the operator who would have little choice in the matter. With more bargaining power, prices could not be imposed on the operator. Management would have to reach agreement.

● Many different unions have members in the engineering industry. There could be at least four, and sometimes up to as many as ten or twelve unions in any one factory. This has tended to encourage the development of shop-stewards and shop-stewards' committees to enable the trade unionists in the workplace to speak with one voice.

These pressures for local bargaining and organization have existed alongside a complicated national structure. National negotiations between the Confederation of Shipbuilding and Engineering Unions (CSEU) and the Engineering Employers' Federation (EEF) set minimum hourly wage rates for the three main categories of manual workers: skilled, semi-skilled, and unskilled. In addition they lay down minimum conditions for holidays, hours of work, overtime and night shift premiums. In the area of wages, national rates rose relatively slowly in the years after the war. Much more progress was made by trade union members and shop-stewards by using negotiations on piece-work to push up actual earnings. These arguments about piece-work often gave a very important role to the shop-steward who would assist the individual worker in settling a price or act as the spokesperson for the group. The gap between national rates and actual earnings grew rapidly, especially in areas such as the West Midlands, where there was an effective shop-steward organization. In recent years, however, as we shall see in Chapter four on living standards, the gap has begun to narrow again.

The other aspect of national bargaining was the procedure agreement between the CSEU and EEF. This laid down the steps to be taken by a union member and the union when they wanted to raise a grievance with the management. This began with the member raising the problem with the foreman and went right through to a national meeting involving EEF and CSEU representatives.

Most workers' grievances arise from actions taken by management. This national procedure allowed management to take action, leaving it up to the worker(s) affected to complain about it by using a process that could easily take six months to work through. Not surprisingly, union members were reluctant to stick to such a drawn out process when they found it possible to resolve problems much more directly. Often, therefore, they applied sanctions before procedure was exhausted. Management responded to this pressure because they wanted to keep production going and gain the cooperation of workers in introducing changes in the workplace. Thus the formal procedure became increasingly out of touch with the real relationships that developed in the workplace. For years the engineering unions tried to persuade the engineering employers to alter the procedure. Finally, they succeeded in 1976 when a 'status quo' clause was written into the national procedure agreement. This meant that management were supposed to gain agreement or themselves exhaust procedure *before* they introduced changes in working conditions.

The response to workplace trade unionism

Resistance to the growth of shop-floor power

The power of the work-group, and their spokesperson, the shop-steward, grew. It was an expression of the gap that existed between the possibilities open to organized workers to win concessions and improvements from their management, and the rigid procedures and agreements they had inherited. This did not, however, take place without any resistance. Much of the popular coverage of industrial relations in the press focussed on the 'irresponsible' role of the shop-steward, often portrayed as wild and dangerous, acting in a subversive fashion. All the publicity was about strikes rather than the day-to-day role of the shop-steward. Both the union leaders and many employers were reluctant to concede too much power and influence to them.

This conflict within the unions was seen most clearly in the largest union in engineering, the Amalgamated Engineering Union (AEU, now the Amalgamated Union of Engineering Workers, AUEW). The AUEW has a democratic formal structure based on the branch to which members living in a particular area belong. The branch participates in elections for the full-time officers at district, divisional and national level. In addition the union's key policy-making bodies, the national committee (an annual conference of fifty-two members elected from divisions) and the executive committee (a full-time body elected from the union's regions) are themselves elected through a branch vote. In recent years this structure has been significantly modified by the introduction of postal ballots.

Within the structure, however, existed (and indeed exists) an informal 'party system' in which left-wing and right-wing groupings contest elections and struggle for control over the union. In some areas like North London, Manchester and Sheffield the left has traditionally been strong whilst others, such as Birmingham and the North East have usually supported right-wing candidates. In the fifties and early sixties, overall control was held by the right wing as they had a majority on the executive committee as well as the key posts of general secretary and president. This leadership frequently came into conflict with the assertive shop-stewards movement. When strikes did take place, they often refused to give support.

One company that was equally determined to prevent the growth of effective shop-steward organization was the motor giant, Ford. They had recognized stewards in the late forties but were keen to restrict their role. Unlike most of the other car companies, there was no piece-work system at Ford. Wages were determined nationally. Ford negotiated with a team of full-time officers, one from each union with members in the combine. When there was a confrontation between the shop-floor organization and the company the union leadership had little sympathy for their members' action.

Ford had taken over the Briggs body plant which supplied body pressings to their nearby Dagenham site. There was a strong shop-steward organization at Briggs and Ford immediately began trying to reduce its influence. The outcome of this conflict was a strike which focussed on the sackings of one of the Briggs convenors. Faced with this, the AEU president stated:

'For a long time now, subversive elements have been at work at Briggs. Last year there were 200 stoppages in the plant. In my view those subversive types were responsible for most, if not all, of them.'

Hugh Beynon *Working for Ford* (EP Publishing)

A similar situation arose at Dagenham five years later in 1962 when the Ford's management sacked seventeen stewards as part of a drive against the shop-floor union organization. Again they were able to rely on the fact that the union nationally would not come to the support of its members and activists at Dagenham.

The conflicts at Ford illustrated two features of the growth of shop-floor power. Firstly many managements resented the challenge to their traditional prerogatives and tried to nip it in the bud. Disputes often took place provoked by the sacking, or attempted sacking, of stewards and convenors. It also illustrated the tensions that this development created within the trade union organization itself. The relationship between the car workers and the AEU was paralleled in many ways with the tense and uneasy relationship between the dockers and their main union, the Transport and General Workers'.

Responsible spokesperson?

Whilst the dramatic conflicts in the car factories and the docks dominated the headlines, they do not tell the whole story of the time. Many employers were willing to tolerate, and at times encourage, the growth of shop-steward organization. The pressures on them to do this were various:

● Direct negotiation with workplace representatives made more economic sense to many engineering employers, some of whom were not noted for their loyalty to the employers' federation. After all the umbrella of the engineering industry covered a range of firms, from a back street employer of ten people supplying washers to a nearby contractor, to a giant multinational firm, controlled from North America and selling on the world market. To attract and retain workers, and secure their cooperation in technical changes, the large employer was willing to deal directly with his employees and probably pay them more than the tiny firm could afford.

● Employers and managers experienced in dealings with shop-stewards rejected in practice the caricature of them as industrial wreckers. They could no longer coerce their employees and found that workplace representatives could play a key role in maintaining the cooperation of workers who were much more confident and demanding than their fathers had been before the war.

● Finally, although steward organization was robust on matters concerning the workplace, its challenge was limited in scope. Generally speaking, stewards did not question the right of the employers to own and control the factories; they just wanted to ensure that the workers were given a good price for their labours.

Many employers were keen to see unions represent all their workers, and deliberately encouraged 100 per cent membership through closed-shop and check-off agreements. This policy made it easier for them to deal with any conflicts in an organized way. Typically, their approach to stewards was different to that displayed at Ford in 1957 and 1965. They were willing to talk to them at the same time as looking at ways through which the stewards' commitment to the firm could be strengthened and their loyalty to their members could be lessened. They were looking for a more stable workplace organization that could be relied upon to deliver the cooperation of the work-force albeit at a price. Some of the steps taken by employers to help push shop-steward organization in this direction were:

● Encouraging stewards to become involved in areas like discipline, redundancy, grading appeals, safety committees, along with regular consultation exercises in which

36

stewards would be given information about the state of production and the order book.

- Trying to introduce detailed written and factory-wide agreements in place of the maze of very informal agreements and understandings that had grown up between individual managers and groups of workers and their stewards.
- Replacing out-of-date procedures that were ignored, by new ones which were more likely to be used by union members.
- Helping the stewards build up a stable and continuous organization by offering them facilities to meet regularly, along with the time off to undertake their duties, a room to work in and sometimes secretarial assistance.

Government policy seemed to support both views of the steward: as a rebel and as a responsible advocate. Thus Barbara Castle's proposals 'In Place of Strife' and the Conservative Industrial Relations Act seemed to contain the assumption that legal constraints were needed on the power of shop-stewards and that power in the union should be shifted back to the full-time officials. At the same time, both governments were putting forward proposals aimed at underpinning the second view. 'In Place of Strife' offered the unions substantial amounts of money to help them 'modernize their operations', to be spent on areas like shop-steward training.

The legislation introduced by the 1974-79 Labour Government moved much further in this direction. Since 1977, stewards and safety representatives have had the legal right to paid time off, both to undertake their role as workplace representatives and to be trained by the unions. Below we can see some contrasting official views of shop-stewards and workplace organization:

1951 *Unofficial leaders in the London Docks.*

It is the contention of the unofficial leaders that they are at heart good trade unionists, who have been compelled reluctantly to resort to unofficial action and to maintain in being their unofficial organization because of the inability or refusal of their respective Unions to pursue wholeheartedly the true interests of port workers. We have met most of these men in the course of our inquiry and we have received a good deal of first hand evidence about their activities. We find their contention utterly unconvincing. It is our belief that those who direct the activities of the unofficial group have no interest whatever in strengthening and reforming the organization of their respective Unions. Indeed many of them do not appear to have taken the trouble to inform themselves about the constitutional workings of the Unions. In our view, they are more concerned to disrupt the workings of the port as often and as seriously as possible than they are to improve dockworkers' conditions.

Unofficial Stoppages in the London Docks. Report of a Committee of Inquiry. Cmnd 8236. HMSO, 1951.

1957 *Shop-steward organization in the motor industry.*

In short it appears to me in the light of the undisputed facts disclosed in this Inquiry that there is a private union within a union, enjoying immediate and continuous touch with the men in the shop, answerable to no superiors and in no way officially or constitutionally linked with the Union hierarchy.

Report of a Court of Inquiry into the causes and circumstances of a Dispute at Briggs Motor Bodies Ltd Dagenham. Cmnd 131 HMSO, 1957.

1968 *Shop-steward: more of a lubricant than an irritant.*

Consequently it is often wide of the mark to describe shop-stewards as 'trouble makers'. Trouble is thrust upon them. In circumstances of this kind they may be striving to bring some order into a chaotic situation and management may rely heavily on their efforts to do so. Both case studies and surveys show that this sort of situation is not uncommon. In addition the shop-floor decisions which generally precede unofficial strikes are often taken against the advice of shop-stewards. Thus shop-stewards are rarely agitators pushing workers towards unofficial action. In some instances they may be the mere mouthpieces of their work groups. But quite commonly they are supporters of order exercising a restraining influence on their members in conditions which promote disorder. To quote our survey of shop-stewards and workshop relations: 'For the most part the steward is viewed by others and views himself, as an accepted, reasonable and even moderating influence; more of a lubricant than an irritant.'

Royal Commission on Trade Unions and Employers Associations 1965–68. Cmnd 3623 HMSO 1968.

1970 *Undermining the role of the foreman.*

These major developments affecting industrial relations are reflected in what we found to be the position of foremen. From below, their power and influence have been challenged by strong groups of workers, some of whom have used their collective strength to establish new practices such as the control of recruitment and of promotion to better paid jobs. The emergence of shop-stewards as the constitutional leaders of the groups supervised by foremen has presented the latter with powerful rivals. From above, the foremen's managerial role has been allowed to decline because the companies have preferred to centralize any confrontations with the unions. As a consequence foremen feel that in practice their role has been curtailed while the trappings of the job are still preserved. Their sense of being abandoned by management springs from a realistic assessment of what they see around them. Groups of workers have taken to themselves some of the supervisors' tasks, and decisions on many day-to-day issues are taken by management at higher levels than the foreman.

> CIR Report No 4   Birmingham Aluminium Casting (1903) Company Ltd, Dartmouth Auto Castings Ltd, Midland Motor Cylinder Company Ltd.
> HMSO Cmnd 4264, HMSO 1970.

1971 *The steward as a 'natural link'*

One of the basic reasons for the steward's existence is to discuss matters with management, whose influence on the steward's behaviour is considerable. Our studies show that by recognizing the positive role the steward may perform management can aid effective industrial relations. The steward generally has intimate knowledge of conditions in the plant and of his members' wishes. Increasingly as firms embark on changes they find it necessary to secure the cooperation of the work-force. As the steward is the representative of his constituency he provides a natural link.

> *Commission on Industrial Relations Report No. 17*
> *Facilities afforded to Shop-Stewards.*
> Cmnd 4668, HMSO 1971.

These changes in management attitudes, along with alterations in areas like payments systems, have helped to radically change the face of workplace trade unionism in the engineering industry. One of the best signs of this is the rapid increase in the number of full-time convenors, or senior shop-stewards. A recent study of this subject says:

'. . . there are approximately 5000 full-time stewards covering manual workers in approximately 3000 manufacturing establishments . . . we feel reasonably confident in concluding that the number of full-time stewards has quadrupled in the last decade.'

'Factors Shaping Shop-Steward Organization in Britain' by William Brown, Robert Ebsworth and Michael Terry in *British Journal of Industrial Relations* July 1978

This was a significant development which helped consolidate workplace organization. It did, however, also lead to complaints that the very close links between stewards working on the job and their members were being weakened.

Shop-steward organization

Convenors in the unions

It was not only industrial management but also trade union officials that altered their attitude to shop-floor leaders, although the process was a complicated one. Within the AEUW which we discussed earlier, many of the convenors in the motor industry played an important part in campaigning for change. When Hugh Scanlon was elected president in 1968 this was a victory for hundreds of stewards and convenors who wanted to see the union take a more positive attitude to workplace organizations and a more supportive approach to the changing demands of the membership. Their enthusiasm for change had helped organize a substantial vote for Scanlon and the other left wing candidates.

The structure of the TGWU is different, their general secretary is elected by a vote of the membership but their other full-time officers are appointed. However, not dissimilar changes took place in their union around the same time after Jack Jones was elected general secretary in 1969. The union pursued the policy of promoting plant bargaining and giving stewards and convenors a greater say in the union's affairs.

Ford provided one of the first opportunities for these new approaches to be put into effect. The wages of all Ford workers are determined annually between Ford's management and a body called the Ford National Negotiation Council. The latter, as we saw earlier, was a committee of eighteen full-time officials, one from each union with members at Ford. By the end of the sixties, Ford's wages were lagging behind those car factories who had exploited local piece-work bargaining such as British Leyland and Rootes. There was considerable pressure to begin bridging the gap. The 1969 pay offer from Ford, however, included what were called 'penalty clauses', that is, employees would lose certain benefits if they were involved in 'unconstitutional action'. The National Negotiation Council accepted the offer but the members, advised by their shop-stewards, rejected it.

This situation brought to the fore the relationship between the membership and their stewards on the one hand and their national officials on the other. The two big unions, AUEW and TGWU, made the strike official and it was settled three and a half weeks later. Following this they insisted that representation on the committee was brought more into line with membership strengths. Both big unions used their extra places to bring in convenors from the Dagenham and Halewood factories.

This was only one example of a greater willingness by unions to admit leading stewards into the national decision-making process. The benefit it brought for the union leaders was that it reduced the tensions within the unions, making leaders more aware of shop-floor opinion. An added intention was to encourage convenors to act in two ways, transmitting membership opinion upwards and leadership policies downwards.

Again the dockers provide a parallel example. In the midst of the turmoil created by the port employers' attempts to introduce containerization, a lot of pressure was put on the TGWU to find ways to integrate dockers' local leaders more effectively into the union's organization.

By the seventies a number of pressures were combining to reduce the conflicts and divisions within the unions as well as to establish workplace representatives more firmly within the industrial relations system. The enhanced role of the convenor expressed both of these trends.

41

White collar stewards?

In the last chapter we saw how the main growth areas for trade unionism has been outside of the manual/manufacturing sector. In industry, for example, there has been a large expansion of white collar employment and union membership. How has their organization at work compared with that of their blue collar colleagues?

In the engineering industry there is an obvious need for workplace representation in staff areas because there is no system of national negotiations. Nearly always, salaries are reviewed annually at the workplace. Some areas, for example, draughtsmen, have long traditions of office representation and workplace negotiation, and as trade unionism in other areas has grown the first role has often been to try to establish agreed salary grades and regular reviews. Representation has therefore tended to follow payment groups. Thus a typical ASTMS group would have grade representatives for the foremen, the laboratory technicians and perhaps the work study engineers. They would meet together to draw up their annual salary claim.

White collar expectations of what a union is supposed to provide are different from those of blue collar workers. The view is less widely held that the union should be democratic and controlled by the members. White collar workers tend to look to their union to provide a service, a source of professional expertise and assistance. Growing quickly, the staff unions have found it easier to change or modify their structures to adapt to changing bargaining needs.

Stewards in the public sector

Another area of radical change has been trade unionism in the public sector, especially local authority workers and ancillary workers in the National Health Service. Stewards were not recognized in local government until 1969 and the National Health Service in 1971, but this last decade has been a baptism of fire. Many of the main disputes in 1970s Britain involved State employees. To explore more fully the impact of militant trade unionism amongst these workers, we need to look firstly at the considerable expansion in their numbers.

The growth of State employment

Today, many trade unionists working in private manufacturing have a picture of public employment as an impersonal office in a large bureaucratic organization. This image is far from the truth. Certainly the expansion of the State has involved some changes that many of us resent and associate with a loss of liberty. But the major areas of growth in jobs has been in necessary social programmes. The jobs which have been created are often low paid and increasingly insecure.

Social programmes, namely education, health and social services, have increased greatly in significance in the past quarter century. People employed in these three services now account for 40 per cent of all public employees in Britain.

Table 2   Public employment for social programmes in Britain

	1976 (in thousands)
Education	1,680
Health	1,193
Social Services	357
Total	3,230

Changes in Public Employment: A Multi-Dimensional Comparative Analysis, Richard Rose, Centre for the Study of Public Policy, 1980.

We are still a long way behind other countries like Sweden and America in the provision of social programmes. By 1976 12 per cent of Britain's work-force was employed in these services. There is a good chance that one of your neighbours or your own family will be employed as a nurse, teacher, hospital cleaner or school caretaker.

Trade unionists have generally campaigned for an expansion of employment in education and health and social services. Why?

● There are more young people requiring education and more older people requiring a greater amount of health care and social services. It may surprise you to know that in the Western world one quarter of each nation is in school! Even if these numbers fall, as they will in the future, there is still a need to improve the quality of education.
● Social policies have changed and with them the demand for resources. For example, the raising of the legal school leaving age in Britain from fourteen in 1944 to sixteen in 1971 required a large number of new teachers.
● A third cause of increase is the greater social demand for more services. This can be seen in the increasing number of young people staying on in school after the age of sixteen. The effect is to create more demand for services.
● Finally, we have the wealth in our society to allow governments to pay for more doctors, social workers, teachers, and the clerical and office staff without whom they could not work.

In effect, upwards of one half of all public employees are providing us with social benefits that many of us may be in danger of taking for granted.

Union membership amongst public sector workers

Public sector workers are likely to be in a union. The rapid growth in public sector employment, where governments have encouraged union membership, has been matched by an increase in union membership. In 1976, 71.6 per cent of all public sector workers were in a union. Unions which recruited solely from among public employees had over four million members.

Table 3 *Membership of major public sector unions 1949–76*

	1949	1966	1976	1976 Women members as a percentage of total membership
NUPE	150,250	248,041	650,530	65
COHSE	51,319	67,588	200,455	70
NALGO	189,261	348,528	683,011	43
NUT	184,100	253,884	289,107	75
NUM	608,835	412,936	259,966	–

Employment and Trade Unionism in the Public Services R. H. Fryer, T. Manson and A. Fairclough (Capital and Class, Spring 1978) and Annual Reports of the TUC.

Table 3 reveals how quickly the major public sector unions have grown. The membership of NUPE, COHSE and NALGO, nearly quadrupling since 1949. Overall this has offset the fall in the traditional unions like the mineworkers, whose membership was halved in the same period.

Union traditions

Secondly, the union traditions of workers in national and local government contrast strongly with those in, for example, the engineering industry, which we looked at earlier in this chapter. In the public sector 90 per cent or more of public employees are subject to agreements which lay down standard conditions of service and rates of pay for a whole service or nationalized industry. This system of bargaining, through Whitley Councils, is highly structured and formalized and has often proved a barrier to effective organization.

Like their colleagues in engineering, unions in the public sector also came to recognize the value of building a strong organization based on the place of work. Until the late 1960s, trade union energies were absorbed almost totally in national negotiations. The advent of local bonus schemes for manual workers in both the NHS and local authorities – a brainchild of the old Prices and Incomes Board, designed to increase pay without increasing costs – has helped foster the growth

45

of workplace steward activity in the public sector. As we saw, local government officially recognized stewards in 1969, closely followed by the NHS who conceded recognition in 1971. The industrial law of the 1970s has put items like dismissal, safety and sick pay more firmly on to the local agenda, and given more scope for stewards to become involved in meaningful negotiations. A report commissioned by NUPE shows that 39 per cent of their branches had no shop-stewards. By 1974 this figure had fallen to only 11 per cent of the branches. Many of these stewards have been at the centre of industrial action which has taken place in many of the public services during the 1970s.

Union militancy

Linked to this, has been an increase in militancy. The jobs and pay of public employees have been in the firing line as successive governments have tried to deal with the economic crisis. The small number of disputes in the 1950s was in marked contrast to the level reached throughout the 1970s. The number of days lost through stoppages was on average four times as great in the 1970s; the number of workers involved in disputes increased threefold and individual strikers lost on average eight days due to strikes as compared to the five days lost in the 1950s. One of the features of the resurgence of industrial unrest has been the reaction of public sector workers to government policy. In each case, apart from the miners, whose previous struggles had taken place when the industry was in private hands, the workers involved had little history of official militancy. Local authority, fire brigade, some post office and Civil Service employees had their first experience of an official countrywide strike. The fact that by 1973 there were major disputes involving the application of incomes policy in three public sector industries – the mines, electricity, and railways – is proof that much of the action was directed against government policy rather than against the immediate employing authority.

Relations with the State

Additionally, what is always conveniently overlooked is that public sector pay and conditions are determined by the government's willingness to advance funds. A major dispute in this sector, therefore, automatically becomes political, however much a government may insist that it is purely a managerial matter. The 1970s saw the emergence of a new generation of public employees who tended to view their often low paid work as a job like any other, to be evaluated by similar criteria and improved by similar methods. The fact that they have found themselves engaged in protracted strikes against the government (acting as both employer and as the State) adds another dimension to the relationship between trade unions and the State.

Women workers

Looking at public sector trade unionism highlights another very important change, the rapid expansion in the number of women trade unionists, as seen in Chapter one. Of course, a lot of trade unionists have always been women. In both world wars, millions of women were brought into the labour force. And women have predominated in many jobs and industries, like clothing and textiles.

More recently though, the expansion of public sector employment has involved the recruitment of many more women workers. Virtually one in three of all women workers are employed in either central or local government, it is not, therefore, surprising that women form the majority of members in public sector unions. Here, as elsewhere, we find few women in positions of authority in either their chosen occupation or their union.

Many women in the public services are not given the opportunity to do well paid jobs. There are a variety of reasons for this. Large numbers of women are forced to work part time or irregular hours in order to combine their jobs with the responsibility of caring for a home and young children. Cleaners in hospitals and government offices work twilight

47

shifts after their husbands have come back from work. Female clerical staff often find employment during school hours. Government estimates suggest that 40 per cent of women work part time. In the public services, women are concentrated in the lowest grades of any pay structure. Even in areas of the professions which women dominate, like primary school teaching and nursing, men get the top jobs. Seventy-five per cent of primary school teachers are women but only one in ten of them is likely to become a head or deputy head. Almost five out of every ten male school teachers rise to the top job. Of course these problems of inequality, low pay and inferior terms of employment are common to women workers in both the public and private sector. In this respect there is no difference between the machinist in the factory or in the office.

Given that the public services are a major employer of female labour we might expect to find their unions dominated by women and women's issues. This is not the case because many of the same difficulties experienced by women in work are carried over into union life. The prejudices of their male colleagues confront them in work and in the union. The domestic pressure of cooking, ironing and looking after children still have to be faced. Men and women may work together during the day but when it comes to the evening it's usually the man who puts his coat on and goes off to the union meeting.

Unions in the public sector face very important challenges. Firstly, they need to ensure that women members play an active part in decision-making. The only way they can achieve this is to adapt their own organization to accommodate the needs of what is, after all, the majority of their membership. There are some signs that this is being done. NUPE has created five seats for women on its national executive. NALGO has a network of equal opportunities committees and a regular equal opportunities bulletin. The NUT has given some full-time officials a special responsibility for women members. The two large general unions with membership in the public sector have recently decided to set up equal rights committees in the regions. The TUC, which has its own womens conference, last year endorsed a ten-point charter aimed at encouraging unions to take positive steps to encourage women's participation. It recommends, where appropriate, women's seats on national and local bodies, special advisory committees, paid time off for union meetings in working hours, childcare arrangements for meetings in working hours, special encouragement for women to attend union training, and non-sexist union publications. There is still a long way to go before changes like these are accepted by the broad union movement.

Issues affecting women trade unionists are at last starting to get on to conference agendas and appear in union journals. The unions did campaign for legislation on equal pay and sex discrimination, neither of which have resulted in very dramatic progress. They are, in fact, an acknowledgement that traditional bargaining has done little to promote equality. Some public employers have become equal opportunity employers and agreed to improved maternity provisions for their female workers. Many of these commitments have been impressive on paper but less so in practice. Furthermore, the policies of the 1979 Conservative Government are reversing many of the gains women have made in recent years. Public sector unions have campaigned on a number of women's issues. NALGO has been at the forefront of the battle for decent nursery facilities. NATFHE (National Association of Teachers in Further and Higher Education, the teachers in many of our colleges) have supported the establishment of childcare facilities at work. NUPE and COHSE have organized a special educational programme for their women members.

Key points

● The growth of workplace bargaining and organization in all major industries is a feature of the post-war years.
● The development of shop-steward organization in engineering often met with stubborn resistance from the offi-

49

cial union leadership and major employers, like for example, Ford.

● The principal job of stewards is to negotiate local rates of pay and handle members' grievances.

● Some employers encouraged the growth of union membership and with it workplace representation as a means of gaining the cooperation of workers in implementing change.

● The growth of a large number of full-time convenors was confirmation of the importance of workplace bargaining and organization to the national trade union movement.

● The experience of workers in white collar jobs and the public sector, led them to adopt similar patterns of organization to those in engineering.

● Representation in unions is still dominated by men even though increasingly high proportions of their membership are women.

Discussion

● How do you see the role of stewards in your place of work?

● What in your experience are the major problems facing workplace trade union organization?

● What steps can be taken to ensure that the interests of women members are more fully represented in your union?

Further reading

Once again, why not start with your own industry and union? Union hand-books for shop-stewards and branch officers will explain your union's organization. Also get hold of the collective agreements covering your workplace. These agreements may be local or national.

Working for Ford (EP Publishing) is a paperback which gives a very full account of the struggle to organize in the car industry.

We ended by posing the question of the organization of women workers. Another book in this series entitled Women at Work, by Chris Aldred (Pan, 1981) expands on many of these important points.

Chapter Three

Unions and the State: cooperation or conflict?

We've looked so far at the ways in which the role of unions at work has changed in recent years. The negotiation of wages and conditions of employment has certainly remained the central focus. But is this the limit of our trade union activity? Should unions be content to negotiate for a membership that is less than a quarter of the population. The answer must be no.

As well as being trade unionists at work, we are also consumers, parents, tenants and householders. Sometimes we're sick or disabled. At times we may be unemployed. And we all hope to live to become old age pensioners. So naturally, the concerns of trade unions stretch outside of the

51

workplace. Recognizing this, the trade union movement's aims include social and economic objectives. The main ones are:

- The provision by the State of a high standard of free education and health care for everyone;
- The protection of the living standards of non-wage earners: old people, one parent families, people who are unemployed;
- The adoption by the government of economic policies that will encourage growth and full employment.

In pursuing these aims, trade unions have used a mixture of collective bargaining and political action.

But the initiative has not come just from the aspirations of trade union members. The state has become much more involved in our relationships at work, for example in trying to control wages and salaries. Unions have had to respond to this kind of development even though they may have often wanted to 'keep out of politics'. Additionally, as the State has become more active in attempting to plan the economy, unions have been encouraged to play a part in this process. A good example of this is the frequent invitations for trade union representatives to sit alongside employer representatives on various government committees.

This chapter will look at trade union involvement with the State in three ways:

- How traditionally trade unions have worked through the parliamentary system to influence State policy. The main method has been their support of the Labour Party.
- How trade unions, normally through the TUC or locally through trades councils, have increasingly been directly represented on a variety of State institutions.
- How through experience in the Labour Party and contact with State institutions union structure has been modified, and they have come to formulate and campaign for their own social and economic policies.

Unions and the Labour Party

The original impetus for independent labour representation in Parliament dates from the beginning of this century. Then as now, unions were fighting oppressive legislation which threatened their very existence. In a famous court case in 1901, known as Taff Vale, the House of Lords decided that the Amalgamated Society of Railway Servants should pay the Railway Company £23,000 damages as a result of a strike. This decision effectively removed the right to strike and convinced many trade unionists that they needed their own voice in Parliament. Unless they could directly influence legislation, they would never be able to protect the industrial interests of their members.

The Labour Party was established as a defensive measure; to look after labour interests in Parliament. It took the form of a federation of different working class organizations: trade unions, the cooperative society and socialist organizations like the Independent Labour Party. It was not until 1917 that people were able to join the party as individuals.

The structure of the Labour Party has changed little since those early days. Unions and Labour are closely linked. In the words of one historian,

The Labour Party is bound to the unions not just by cash and card votes, but by personalities and doctrines, common experience, sentiment and mutual advantage.

As by far the largest affliliated organizations, trade unions have most of the votes in the party's formal decision-making organizations: the annual conference and the national executive committee. Figure 5 shows how Labour and union organization overlaps at national and local levels.

But the fact that trade unions have most of the votes in the party's formal structure does not mean that they control it. Firstly, the trade unions that are affiliated to the Labour Party (and some big unions are not) rarely agree on policy matters. The usual pattern has been for different unions to support different sections of the parliamentary leadership. So union votes often cancel each other out. But there is a

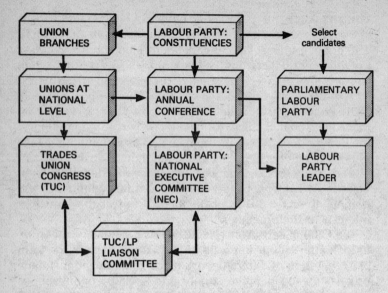

Figure 5 Union links with the Labour Party

second, more deeply rooted reason. Because Labour is a parliamentary party, real power, especially during periods of Labour Government lies with the Labour Members of Parliament and particularly the Cabinet and the Prime Minister. Despite their strong organizational links, trade unions have usually found that they are just one source of pressure on a Labour government. Frequently this leads to conflicts between Labour and the unions.

Labour in office

There were two short-lived minority Labour governments in the 1920s but the first majority Labour government took office straight after the war. As we saw earlier, there had been a massive expansion of planning during the war. Rationing, conscription of labour and legal bans on strikes had been used as part of the drive to mobilize national resources for the war effort. Politicians of all the major parties agreed after the war that the state still had a central role to play in post-

54

war reconstruction. The new Labour Government took a number of steps in this direction with the enthusiastic backing of the trade union movement. A number of important basic industries were nationalized and the Welfare State was radically expanded, especially in the areas of health, with the formation of the National Health Service, education and social services. Both major parties agreed too that it was the government's responsibility to plan the economy to ensure that there would never be a return to mass unemployment.

Despite a large popular vote, Labour lost the election in 1951 which ushered in thirteen years of Conservative rule. Out of office, Labour maintained its close institutional links with the trade unions, in fact the number of trade unionists paying the political levy (most of which went to the Labour Party) went up considerably. But there were a number of signs that the enthusiastic support of trade unionists for the party which had existed in 1945 was waning. The Labour vote declined. The number of trade unionists who joined the Labour Party as individual members fell. There is a lot of local evidence to suggest that involvement of trade unionists, especially manual workers, in local party organization, also became less significant. Some of the implications of this growing rift revealed themselves when Labour next took office in 1964.

An uneasy alliance?: the Labour Government 1964–70

Although the living standards of most working-class people had risen considerably by the mid-sixties, there were signs that the boom was coming to an end. Harold Wilson, Labour's new leader was quick to seize upon Britain's comparatively slow rate of growth as a reason for decline. Furthermore, unemployment had once again begun to rise. Trade unionists, especially those working in the State service sector, were aware that poverty, poor housing and unequal access to education still persisted on a massive scale. It was obvious that the Welfare State was not working.

The experience of the 1964–70 Labour Government did little to improve working class living standards or alter basic inequalities. Wilson's attempts to manage the economy during a growing economic crisis increasingly drew the Government into conflict with the trade union movement. Government attempts to control wages were the major source of this conflict. The unions saw measures which they expected from Conservative governments being pressed on them by a government of their own choosing. The seamen's dispute in May 1966 provided an example of the unions' inability to influence a Labour government. The seamen had recognized that they were required to work nearly fifty-six hours a week when at sea and they were now pressing for a forty-hour week with no reduction in their basic rate. Conflict was inevitable. The Government was unconcerned with the merit of the seamen's case but worried about the damage the claim might do to the prices and incomes policy.

What is at issue here is our national prices and incomes policy. To accept the demand would be to breach the dykes of our prices and incomes policy . . . Our determination to insist on these principles when the cost is great will be taken by everyone at home and abroad as a proof of our determination to make that policy effective. (Harold Wilson television broadcast)
Paul Foot *The Politics of Harold Wilson* (Penguin)

The strike was pictured as a strike against the State and community as well as the ship owners. Tremendous pressure, including the notorious allegation that the strikers were being manipulated by a 'tightly-knit group of politically motivated men' was put on the seamen to get them back to work. This was to be the first of a number of clashes between groups of trade unionists and the Labour Government.

The conflicts that took place over incomes policy, and later in 1969 over Barbara Castle's attempt to restrict unions rights in 'In Place of Strife' were seen as damaging both by Labour and trade union leaders. In 1972 a TUC–Labour Party liaison committee was formed to help repair this damage. Trade union leaders felt that these conflicts could be avoided if they had a greater say in the development of Labour Party policies. Opposition to the policies of the Heath Government brought union and party leaders closer together. The Industrial Relations Act and attempts at wage control policies both provoked powerful opposition. The TUC coordinated a campaign of opposition to the Industrial Relations Act which led to unions being expelled for breaking ranks and registering under the Act. It was resistance to incomes policy, most spectacularly from the miners, that led to the downfall of the government.

The 1974 election was fought on the issue of trade union power. Heath tried to build up a popular hostility to the trade union movement on the theme: who runs the country? Labour and the TUC responded in 1975 with a social contract between government and trade unionists designed to greatly reduce conflict in industry. The key to the agreement was trade union support for wage restraint in exchange for much greater consultation on social and economic matters. Certainly the visible relations between party and union leaders were radically different from 1964–70 and a great deal of industrial legislation was introduced which had the support of the trade unions.

However, the significance of the social contract period was not just that it represented a closer relationship between Labour and the unions. It also encouraged a much greater direct trade union involvement with the State.

The growing State

Support for the Labour Party was the most important and popularly understood way in which trade unionists have tried to influence political events. But on its own it was insufficient. We have seen how trade union involvement in the Labour Party did not prevent collisions between the two during the period of the 1964–70 Government. It was the same issue, incomes policy, which strained the social contract to breaking point towards the end of 1978. There are other reasons why unions would not want to restrict their efforts to working within the Labour Party. The Labour Party has been in opposition for roughly half the period we are considering and trade unions have had to deal with Conservative governments. Secondly, many trade union members are not Labour supporters and some unions, including large ones like NALGO and the NUT, are not themselves affiliated to the party. All these trade union members need some political representation. There is a third reason, however, why the trade union movement had adopted a broader view of political influence. Involvement in the Labour Party enabled trade unionists to have some influence in Parliament. But increasingly the activities of a wider range of State institutions were having an important effect on peoples' lives at work.

Unions have always been portrayed as actively seeking political power. This is, as we've seen, partly true. However, the growth of the state has involved trade unionists in new forms of political activity. Union participation in the state has both benefits and drawbacks as the following four examples show.

The State as employer

The willingness of governments to control the living standards of their own employees has been a feature of government policies since the sixties. The interests of workers in the public sector have been subordinate to the demands of economic management. Recurrent attempts to cut public expenditure have created redundancies and led to job insecurity. The three out of ten workers who are State employees have found negotiations about their own wages being used as a means of influencing settlements in the private sector. Understandable resistance from unions like NALGO, NUPE and the Fire Brigade Union is often interpreted as being a political challenge to government. The extracts opposite from the popular press illustrate the type of violent response that normal industrial action by public sector workers can generate.

The machinery of economic planning

In common with other industrialized countries, the State in Britain has taken an increasing role in economic planning.

(Glasgow)

Jan 31 1979: "Unions set to tighten the screw"

GLASGOW HERALD

Jan 20 1979: "Scotland is bracing itself over the weekend for Black Monday when..."

The Northern Echo

Jan 29 1979: "More hardship is on the cards from today as hospital and council workers threaten the big squeeze if they don't get their way over pay."

YORKSHIRE POST

Jan 23 1979: "Lives at risk as strikers show no mercy."

The Star
(Sheffield)

Jan 23 1979: "Sheffield tonight is a city of complete industrial chaos as more bodyblows from the unions pound home."

Manchester Evening News

Feb 19 1979: "Carry on striking call to bin men."

Evening News

Jan 31 1979: "Town Hall workers have vowed to step up disruptive action."

Evening Post
Lancashire

Jan 30 1979: "Hospital workers tighten noose."

EVENING POST
(Nottingham)

Jan 17 1979: "Life in Strikers' hands."

OBSERVER
(South Bucks)

Feb 2 1979: "Next week the teeth of union power will sink deeper and entire wards will close."

EVENING POST
(Bristol)

Feb 2 1979: "Avon's 2,000 guardian angel nurses today came to the rescue of patients hard hit by the intensifying campaign of disruption by hospital ancillary workers."

The reader needs to go no further than these snippets to discover the attitude of the newspapers concerned to the disputes to which they refer.

Source: *A cause for concern: Media coverage of industrial disputes, January–March 1979* (TUC)

This has accelerated since the beginning of the sixties. A feature of government planning has usually been the involvement of trade union representatives alongside employers and government representatives. 1962 marked a turning point when the Conservative Government established the National Economic Development Council. This body of employer, union and government representatives was designed to set targets for economic growth and identify the obstacles in the way of achieving them. Since these first attempts at planning, a large number of joint committees have been established in different industries.

Economic planning has also involved a more direct role for the State in the management of particular industries. As we saw, in 1945 the newly elected Labour Government, with the support of the unions, embarked on a period of planned nationalization. By 1970 transport and communications, coal and steel, in addition to the public utilities like gas, water and electricity were in public ownership. In the seventies, the State became an employer of last resort, as the failures of private enterprise, like Rolls-Royce and British Leyland, came under its control. This pressure to save and create jobs was behind a new planning initiative, the National Enterprise Board, launched by Labour in 1975. It was given the power to lend money to companies for investment or itself to obtain a controlling share in private firms and encourage the signing of planning agreements. In this way old firms like Alfred Herberts (the machine tool company) and new electronic specialists like ICL and INMOS received public funds.

The idea of a much more active State role in trying to promote industrial growth through the new National Enterprise Board and planning agreements was one of the main policies that came out of the TUC–Labour Party Liaison committee. TUC representatives served on the board of the National Enterprise Board. However, the TUC was disappointed that the amount of money available to the NEB remained small and only one employer, the American car firm, Chrysler, entered into a planning agreement. The experience of trade union members in firms that came under the control of the NEB were often extremely critical of its approach. They found its priorities often centred around rationalization and cutting jobs, an approach often harsher than that adopted by their former private owners.

State involvement has not simply meant nationalization. Between 1963 and 1973 alone private firms received government help of £6000 million, compared with £4000 million received by nationally-owned industries. These grants, loans and subsidies have gone to every industry, from the multinational car giant, Chrysler, to individual farmers. Successive governments have used financial incentives to tempt employers to those regions worst hit by the loss of jobs in basic industries like coal, steel and shipbuilding.

Attempts by the State to control wages

We've already seen how the attempts of the State to 'plan' wages proved the main pressure point between government and unions in three successive governments. Particularly during a period of Labour government, strong pressures were put on the TUC to accept, or at least acquiesce in, wage controls. In 1948, for example, the Labour Government, under Attlee, succeeded in winning the cooperation of the TUC for a wage freeze. The TUC in turn effectively held the freeze for more than two years. In 1965, the TUC established an Incomes Policy Committee to vet the claims of its members, largely in order to forestall the introduction of statutory powers, being threatened by the Labour Government. After 1974, the TUC cooperated in three years of wage controls in exchange for government support in other areas.

However, TUC support for wage controls has invariably caused serious divisions within the trade union movement. In 1967, for example, the TUC Congress reversed the agreement on wage restraint which had the support of its general secretary, George Woodcock. The same Congress went one stage further and by a majority of more than one million votes condemned the government for its 'intervention in collective bargaining as a solution to the country's economic problems'. Eleven years later, it was grass roots opposition

61

that ensured the end of trade union cooperation with Labour's incomes policies.

The State as legislator

Another significant change has been the rapid growth of labour law. Until the mid 1960s there was very little detailed legislation dealing with industrial relations. Since then every government has seen legislation as an important part of its attempts to control industrial relations. In these years, legislation has been introduced on redundancy, unfair dismissals, union recognition, contracts of employment, equal pay, sex discrimination and many other aspects of workplace industrial relations. Often trade unionists have welcomed these developments, seeing them as offering a 'floor of rights' which union negotiators could expand upon through negotiations with employers. In practice, however, they have often proved disappointing. The law on recognition proved helpless in the face of employers who were determined not to recognize a union. Unfair dismissals legislation usually offered a modest amount of financial compensation when the traditional trade union aim had always been the reinstatement of a victimized member. Some people went further and felt that this range of laws was having a damaging effect, weakening the willingness of trade union members to resolve their problems collectively. The use of the law was offering a 'soft option'.

Much more controversial were government attempts to use the law to weaken the right to strike. Union resistance was strong to the proposals to impose compulsory 'cooling off periods' contained in Labour's 'In Place of Strife', to the concept of the 'unfair industrial practice' included in the Industrial Relations Act and to the severe restrictions on picketing that form a central part of the 1980 Employment Act.

The expansion of labour legislation had three main effects on trade unionists. Firstly it has encouraged trade union members on many occasions to see whether they can resolve a problem through the use of the law. Often this has reduced industrial militancy. An important case in point is the Redundancy Payments Act; the impact of this on trade union resistance to redundancy is discussed in Chapter five. Secondly it led to a further involvement of trade unionists in State institutions. Industrial tribunals were first established in 1964; by the seventies they were a familiar part of the industrial relations scene dealing with large numbers of cases under a variety of different Acts of Parliament. Finally, the use of the law has sometimes had the effect of galvanising general trade union opposition to government policy. There have been very few political strikes in recent British history. Most of them took place as part of the trade union campaign of opposition to the 1971 Industrial Relations Act.

Political influence and trade union organization

Looking through these examples of the increasing interaction between the State and trade unions, we can see some of the ways in which it is affecting trade union organization. One is the increasing representation of trade unionists on State institutions. A number of examples have been given such as the National Economic Development Council and the National Enterprise Board. In the 1970s a number of other new institutions were set up like the Manpower Services Commission, the Health and Safety Commission and the Advisory Conciliation and Arbitration Service (ACAS). All of these include the principle of trade union representation.

This pattern also exists at a local and regional level. If you attend your union branch you may hear reports from the branch's trades council delegate. Trades councils are the way through which the trade union movement is represented on the local State bodies. Delegates are elected to become school and college governors, members of area health authorities and community health councils as well as members of bodies like supplementary benefits appeals tribunals.

To get a clearer picture of this side of the relationship between unions and the State, let's look at an example of one particular service, the health service. See Figure 6.

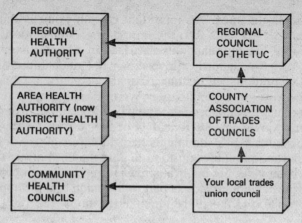

Figure 6   Health and Union representation.

One important thing to remember is that union representation, in this example, is not based on representatives from workers in the health service. Representation and negotiation are deliberately kept quite separate when trade unionists deal with the State. It is little wonder that many trade unionists feel that they lack any real influence in this representative role.

A stronger TUC?

Throughout this discussion we've invariably looked at the role of the TUC rather than (say) the individual union of which you are a member. Why is this? The reason is that the TUC has over the last thirty years succeeded in acquiring a monopoly of the channels of communication with government. Invitations to represent the trade union movement on government committees are sent to the TUC and through its structure an individual trade unionist is chosen. This coordinating role has helped the TUC become more representative than it has ever been in all of its 112 years of existence. Unions have seen the positive advantages of speaking to government and have joined the TUC in order to do this. Today, all significant unions are affiliated, even those who had previously been prevented, like the civil service unions, or those who had at first opposed membership, like NALGO.

But how strong is the TUC? How much authority does it have to speak on behalf of individual unions? Although the TUC now speaks for its member unions on a broad range of national issues, each union retains full authority to represent its members in negotiation with employers. Unions have been reluctant to concede too much of their own power to a central body over which they have less control. A good illustration of this is the fact that the funds made available to the TUC from unions is still quite small. In 1976, for instance, the 115 member unions contributed £1,705,906 to the TUC by way of affiliation fees. This amount is small compared to the budget of the Confederation of British Industry (CBI, the employers' organization) or even your local district council. This shortage of funds has restricted the ability of the TUC to expand its services and its full-time staff.

Most of the pressures which the TUC can apply to a particular union are informal. But unions have been expelled from membership, seventeen were expelled for registering under the 1971 Industrial Relations Act. Perhaps the most potent part of this threat is that, once expelled, unions are no longer protected by the Bridlington procedure. This inter-union agreement bars unions recruiting in areas covered by other TUC-affiliated unions. Unions outside of the TUC have no redress against a TUC affiliate who decides to recruit from amongst their membership.

Whilst the TUC is much less powerful than most people probably think, there are signs that it has begun to take a more central role within the movement.

● Under pressure from the State, the TUC has tried to influence and modify union behaviour for example by setting up procedures to reduce inter-union disputes and to enable expelled members to appeal against expulsion.
● The effect of incomes policy has, as we have seen, been to limit the negotiating freedom of individual unions and groups of workers. There have also been limits on the ability of the TUC, on its side, to agree to incomes policies when confronted by resistance in its own ranks.

● The TUC's own organization has expanded. A good example of this is the growth of the TUC education service which only began life in 1964. The service now offers a massive nationwide programme of courses. It is interesting, too, that this expansion has taken place on the basis of State funding rather than through increased contributions from members. Unions are currently discussing proposals to improve the TUC's services which would include more expansion of education as well as a growth in TUC regional organization.

The development has not just involved changes in structure, but also the development of TUC policies.

A union voice on social and economic policies

It was seen how working through the Labour Party alone did not meet the growing trade union pressures for different social and economic policies. Increasingly the trade unions, through the TUC, have established direct contracts with the State. Additionally, stagnation in industry and cuts in public expenditure, have made it more important for a trade union voice to be heard on social and economic policies. These attacks could not be countered through collective bargaining alone. In response to this, the TUC, has been the forum for the development of detailed and comprehensive policies. Since 1968, the TUC has produced an annual Economic Review, offering a range of policies which union representatives involved in dealing with the state could put forward. Briefings have been provided for unions in different sectors of industry to assist both in bargaining and in involvement in planning.

It is likely that the role of the TUC in campaigning for its own alternative economic strategy will become more important. Part of the current discussion within the unions is about how these policies can be much more widely publicized at all levels, from representatives on national institutions to trades council delegates and ordinary members of the shopfloor.

Key points

● Unions have sought political influence to help achieve their social and economic aims.
● The State has become increasingly involved in collective bargaining; a process trade unionists have often resisted.
● Trying to influence Parliament by supporting the Labour Party has been the main political activity of trade unionists.
● The growth of the State as employer, attempting to plan the economy and to control wages, and as a legislator has greatly increased union contact with the State and its institutions.
● This has led to a slow centralization of power within the trade union movement.
● Increasingly the TUC has acted as the main vehicle for a comprehensive range of trade union social and economic policies.

Discussion

● Are you involved in the Labour Party or the local trades council?
● How successful do you think unions have been in trying to influence government policies?
● Would you like to see the trade union movement become more centralized?

Further reading

As this chapter has shown, most unions look to the TUC to present its alternative policies to government. The most recent and comprehensive statement is found in 'Plan For Growth', the 1981 TUC Economic Review available from the TUC, Congress House, Great Russell Street, London WC1.

A recommended read on workers' experience of the State's involvement in their industries is contained in *State Intervention in Industry: a Workers' Inquiry*. It is published by four trades councils and is available from 5 Queens Street, Newcastle upon Tyne.

Colin Crouch's Book, *The Politics of Industrial Relations* (Fontana) offers a hard but worthwhile read on the subject.

Some usetul hints on how to go about influencing the political process are contained in a book by Ann Taylor and Jim Fryth, *Political Action*. This is one of a series of books published by Arrow books on trade union subjects.

Chapter **Four**

Improved Standards of Living?

Reg was involved in some tricky negotiations with Ford some years ago. There came a point in the talks when they started to wheel out a few goodies. One apparently was funeral benefits. After a little while there was a knocking under the table. Everyone looked round in surprise, even his own colleagues. It was Reg who was doing the knocking. 'What on earth's the matter?' asked the management. Reg looked up at the ceiling: 'I'm speaking to my members who have passed on. They're asking if you can make those payments retrospective. . .'

(Keith Harper, 1977 TUC Conference)

Even the dead wish to preserve their standards of living! The struggle to achieve this single objective, of protecting and improving our living standards, unites us to our unions. It is the major reason why we become members. Our pursuit of this objective, through the unions, has continued to be a cause of conflict and tension in the post-war years. In this chapter we examine why this should be the case. Our themes come in the form of answers to five questions:

● What is our standard of living and how do we measure it?
● Where does our standard of living come from?
● How have trade unions tried to control our living standards?
● Why have unions experienced difficulty in maintaining our standard of living?
● Is there any conflict over living standards?

What is our standard of living and how do we measure it?

Changing standards of living

Standards of living are not easy to define. Most of us look for a material improvement, which we measure in the amount of money we earn. Usually, this priority is set above all others.

Many knew that in the long run their plants would close, that their health would suffer, that their strength would wane. But who could tell? And what could be done about it? These were not urgent questions; the job would be there there tomorrow, and the money. T. Nichols and P. Armstrong – *Workers Divided* (Fontana, 1976)

If the views of these chemical workers are correct, then the possession of a job and pay packet should guarantee a decent standard of living. But is this necessarily true? Take, for example, the findings of two recent research studies. One concluded that in 1976, those of us in full-time employment were three times as affluent as our grandfathers. In complete contrast to this, another researcher argued that as many as fourteen million of us, that's 26 per cent of this country's population, are living in or near poverty. One says we're rich, the other says we're poor, and they are both right. If we measure the quality of life just in terms of pay then we are better off than previous generations. If, however, we include other incomes like the value of our house or car, public services and employment benefits in our view of living standards then the picture changes. Even with these additional resources we don't all enjoy the same standard of living. What we can buy, the activities we can undertake are only in part dependent on our pay packet. Many of those in poverty are not working, they are unemployed, retired or single parents. Many of those near poverty are in low paid jobs.

So, to recap, we measure our standard of living primarily in terms of pay and what it will buy, but other sources of income are important. You may earn exactly the same as the person working next to you, but that doesn't mean you will enjoy the same standard of living.

Similarly, we do not have a fixed view about what our standard of living should be. Our demands reflect the times in which we live. In 1957, for instance, we might have agreed with the then Prime Minister who said that most people had 'never had it so good'. By comparison with the economic depression of the thirties and the austerity of wartime Britain, the relative peace and prosperity of the late fifties was an improvement. But even then we could not have fully appreciated what was to follow: the growth of the 'mass consumer age' with the family car, television, supermarkets, synthetic fibres and washing machines. To us in the eighties these former luxury items appear as necessary parts of our material standard of living. We have constantly adjusted our definition of the standard of living in order to keep pace with the economic, technical and social changes of the last three decades.

We have channelled these demands for a more or less continuous improvement in our standard of living through the unions. They have responded, wherever possible, by seeking increases in wages to match these demands. In order to achieve these gains unions have bargained with employers. Unions realize that it is negotiation on wages that has the most immediate impact upon their members' living standards. Their short term goal is, understandably, to maximize the financial benefits of every individual bargain. Since 1945, the definition of those 'financial benefits' has broadened considerably, as unions and their members have adjusted their bargaining priorities, in line with changes in the style and cost of living.

Let's take as an example the views of the former miner, printed opposite, who, when interviewed, was working on the surface as a fork-lift truck driver. This particular interview was given in evidence to the Wilberforce Inquiry into pay in the coal industry in 1972. He was questioned by Lawrence Daly representing the union and two members of the Inquiry team. What he had to say tells us a lot about what goes to make our standard of living.

This ex-miner, whose job had ruined his health, had been redeployed and taken a substantial cut in earnings. Faced with the alternative of working above ground at the pit or in a local factory, he chose the pit. He was not making his decision just on what he could earn. He had turned down a chance of a £30-a-week job. If he left the pit other things would be lost, his pension, concessionary coal and extra holidays. These were obviously an important element in his standard of living.

Is it the same for you? What makes up your standard of living?

In the last thirty years the extension of collective bargaining has enabled trade unionists to share with management in decision-making on these other issues, namely, the hours and conditions of work, pensions, holidays and the methods of wage payment. For a fuller account of the role trade unions can play in decision-making with management, see a companion volume in this series: *Democracy at Work*.

Measuring living standards

What we earn from work remains our primary concern, but the time it takes to earn and spend that money, and the

Daly: Have you ever worked underground?

Witness: Yes, up to 1950.

Daly: Can you explain why you came up to work on the surface?

Witness: I came up with chest trouble, and I could not go down again.

Daly: What would be the reduction in your earnings when you were forced, because of your chest condition, to come from underground up to the surface job, roughly?

Witness: Oh, I was a face-worker at the time.

Daly: You were a face-worker up to 1950?

Witness: Yes.

Daly: I appreciate that it is a long time to remember back, but there would be, I think, at that time as well as today, a very substantial reduction in your earnings because of your chest condition?

Chairman: We can assume that there would be a reduction, yes.

Garnett: As a 'truck driver' – that means as a lorry driver, does it?

Witness: No, a fork-lift truck driver.

Daly: Do you live in a council house?

Witness: Yes.

Daly: He has a take-home pay of £15 per week. Of that £15, what do you pay for rent.

Witness: Just over £3 per week.

Daly: And, although you are a fork-lift truck driver, you have no differential for that skill at all, you are on the minimum rate in the mining industry?

Witness: On the minimum, Grade 2.

Hunter: How does that £15 compare with what might be obtained by a fork-lift truck driver in factories nearby to your area?

Witness: The difference?

Hunter: Yes, in terms of basic rates?

Witness: Well, it is different in different firms, is it not? I would get, I should think, about £30 per week.

Garnett: Why don't you leave and get that job?

Witness: Because I have so much to lose if I leave the colliery.

Garnett: What would you lose?

Witness: Well, my pension and so on.

Garnett: Could you go on a bit about the 'and so on'?

Witness: Well, there is my pension, concessionary coal, there are more holidays – with the rest-days that is; I get more pay for rest-days than I do when I am working, which is true.

Garnett: Could you just explain that to me?

Witness: When we are on holiday, the surface workers and the day-wage workers, we earn more money for holidays than what we have when we are working.

Extract from *A Special Case? Social Justice and the Miners* – J. Hughes and R. Moore (Penguin, 1972) income we can look forward to on retirement are now part and parcel of our standard of living. The ability of unions to bargain about these wider issues is both a measure of their own influence and the importance which we attach to hours, holidays and pensions. Progress in these areas gives some indication of changes in our living standards.

Wages Let's begin by looking at the yearly increases which have taken place in the hourly rate of pay for male manual (blue collar) workers. This agreed 'rate for the job' is one measure we use to assess what we can earn.

Table 4 Average rate of change in hourly wage rates

	percentage change
1946–56	6.3
1957–67	4.8
1968–78	13.4

Source: *British Labour Statistics and Historical Abstract, 1886–1968* and *Department of Employment Gazette.*

The first thing we notice is that the average rate of change has fluctuated greatly since 1945. In the middle of our period, the rate of increase declined, only to rise dramatically in later years. Of course, averages mask a wide variation that occurs between individual years. Every year saw an increase in the hourly rates of pay, but they ranged from a low of 1.1 per cent in 1959 to a high of 25.4 per cent in 1975. The seventies, which heralded a decade of two-figure pay increases, would on the surface appear a time of real progress.

Let's look at this later period in a little more detail, this time with the help of a different measure. While the change in hourly rates is important, they do not in themselves determine the values of what we earn. The majority of us judge the value of our earnings by the amount of money which we take home in the pay packet or deposit in the bank at the end of the month. If we add other items, like the weekly child benefit to our take-home pay we have an idea of our real earnings. We still don't know what this will buy because prices increase as well. Maybe an illustration will make this clearer.

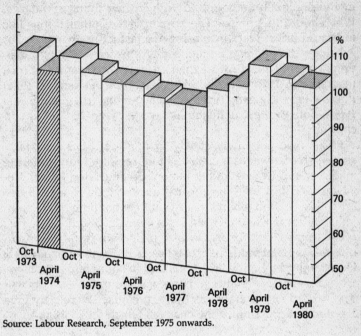

Source: Labour Research, September 1975 onwards.

Figure 7 Changes in real take-home pay

The graph in Figure 7 is an index of take-home pay, which excludes all deductions such as tax and national insurance and includes items like child benefit. It also takes account of the rise in prices during the last five years. This time the earnings of male blue and white collar workers have been included. In 1974, real take-home pay stood at £35.81 per week. This is our base year which on the graph is equal to 100. What the graph shows is how real take-home pay in 1974 compares to the other years. In October 1975, for example, the index stood at 99 which means that our pay was worth less than it was in April 1974.

Remember previously we saw that during the mid-seventies, 1974–6, the hourly rate of pay for blue collar workers was increasing in leaps and bounds. The graph shows that during those same years the real value of their take-home pay was actually falling, and with it their living standards. Why should this be so? The answer is that other things like taxes and prices were increasing at a faster rate than pay: For example, the average family, a man, his wife and two children, paid 19 per cent of their income in tax and national insurance in 1970; this had increased to 24 per cent by 1976. Prices were increasing three times faster than they had in the 1960s. Both of these items, unlike wages, were beyond union control.

Prices rose extremely slowly in the late fifties and early sixties, so real wages increased more rapidly. Only from the mid-sixties onwards did inflation become significant. Between 1966 and 1976 real income increased by roughly 1 per cent a year. Although unions, through bargaining, were gaining significant wage increases, between 1973 and 1980 average earnings before deductions increased from £41.90 to £101.40, the real value of those wages remained unchanged. Our standard of living stood still and in some cases declined. Obviously the experience of particular groups of workers will have varied considerably as the figures used here only give a general impression of the changes which took place.

Hours of work   We have two ways of assessing how many hours we work in an average week. Firstly, we can look at our collective agreement and see what unions and management have agreed is to be the working week. Secondly, we can look at our pay slip and see how many hours we actually worked. Since the early 1950s, when the standard working week was forty-four hours, unions have negotiated a gradual reduction in the basic working week. By the late 1970s the standard being established through collective bargaining was thirty-nine hours per week. There has also been a reduction in the actual number of hours worked, as the graph in Figure 8 indicates.

In 1951, a man with a full-time manual job worked on average forty-eight hours a week. By 1978, this had fallen to

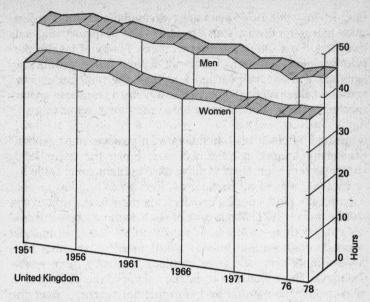

Actual hours worked by men aged 21 and over and women aged 18 and over in full-time manual work

Source: Social Trends No 10, Central Statistical Office, 1979.

Figure 8   Average weekly hours of work: men and women, 1951–78

forty-four hours, though there had been fluctuations during the intervening years. At the same time, the average weekly hours worked by women in employment fell from forty-one hours to thirty-eight hours a week.

The discrepancy between the basic working week and the actual hours worked is explained in a single word, overtime. Male workers in the manufacturing industries have come to rely on overtime payments to maintain their living standards. In 1951, just over 21 per cent of operatives in manufacturing were working on average eight hours overtime a week; by 1978, 34 per cent of all operatives were working an additional eight and a half hours per week. The prevalence of overtime working is not confined to the manufacturing sector, and is also much in evidence in the lowest paid areas of the public sector. In April 1979, even after excessive overtime, groups like manual railway staff, public road transport and bus workers, Post Office manual workers, National Health Service maintenance staff, ambulance drivers and local authority manual workers still earned less than the national average gross weekly pay of £93 per week. Overtime for these groups is clearly being worked in order to provide a living wage.

Holidays Before 1940, holidays with pay were not general, especially among manual workers. Since the early 1950s progress has been fairly steady, as is evident from Table 5.

In 1961, almost all manual workers were entitled to only two weeks paid holiday a year. This increased through the 1960s and by 1971 67 per cent of such workers were entitled to at least three weeks holiday. By 1979, nearly all manual workers had a basic holiday entitlement of at least three weeks (and over half were entitled to four or more weeks holiday). There was also some narrowing of the difference in allowances for manual and non-manual workers, over the period. The increased priority given to holidays in collective bargaining is illustrated by the fact that the number of workers given extra entitlements for length of service has more than doubled in the 1970s, from 17 per cent in 1972 to 38 per cent in 1979.

Pensions We all contribute to our own pensions, which are a form of enforced saving, money set aside that can be spent when retirement age is reached. Some of us contribute to a scheme run by the employer, others rely on the basic state pension.

In order to be entitled to a pension we have to contribute a fair portion of our earnings over a lengthy period of time. The pay slip shown on page 80, which is for a month, shows just how significant that contribution can be. This particular worker had to give up 5 per cent of his income in return for a pension. But then, this white collar worker is relatively fortunate, he at least has a pension scheme. Many of his blue collar counterparts will have fared less well. The need to protect living standards, when employment finishes, has in-

Table 5 Paid holidays: manual employees

United Kingdom

Percentages

Percentage of full-time manual employees entitled to annual paid holidays of duration:

	Under 2 weeks	2 weeks	Between 2 and 3 weeks	3 weeks	Between 3 and 4 weeks	4 weeks and over	All full-time manual employees
1951	31	66	2	1	–	–	100
1961	–	97	2	1	–	–	100
1966	–	63	33	4	–	–	100
1971	–	28	5	63	4	–	100
1972	–	8	16	39	33	4	100
1973	–	6	9	36	45	4	100
1974	–	1	1	30	40	28	100
1975	–	1	1	17	51	30	100
1976	–	1	1	18	47	34	100
1977	–	–	1	18	47	34	100
1978	–	–	1	17	47	35	100
1979	–	–	1	7	42	50	100

Figures are at end-December. The information relates to basic entitlements in national collective agreements of Wages Council orders. Some employees have additional entitlements based on length of service and company agreements; about 38 per cent of employees had such additional entitlements in 1979.

Source: Social Trends No 11, Central Statistical Office, 1981.

TAX CODE AND BASIS	PENSIONABLE PAY	TOTALS THIS YEAR TO DATE			PAY PERIOD ENDING	CODE
		TAXABLE PAY	TAX	SUPERANNUATION	NATIONAL INSURANCE	
073L NORMAL M/W 1	1029.00	954.39	247.45	59.81	31 DEC 76	3
					57.29	

| NORM. HRS. | OV/T HRS. | BASIC PAY OR PENSION | | | | TOTAL GROSS PAY OR PENSION |
| | | 257.25 | ADDITIONS (SEE OVER FOR CODES) | | | 257.25 |

HOURLY RATE

| INCOME TAX | NATIONAL INSURANCE | OTHER DEDUCTIONS (SEE OVER FOR CODES) | | | | TOTAL DEDUCTIONS |
| 59.50 | 14.15 | DI | 1.21 | SB | 11.10 | 100.47 |

SUPERANNUATION

14.51

NET PAY

£156.78

See text on page 78 under 'Pensions'.

volved trade unions in agitating for improvements in the basic State pension and negotiating occupational schemes with the employer.

For most of the 8.5 million people now over pensionable age, retirement is not, financially speaking, a bed of roses. In 1958, 20 per cent of retirement pensioners were on national assistance. Ten years later, the proportion had risen to nearly 29 per cent (by then national assistance had become supplementary benefit). By 1978, it had fallen back to 22.3 per cent with a growing number of the 'young elderly' raised above the poverty line by occupational pensions. From 1948 to 1978, the State scheme changed remarkably little. The basic pension rose from £1.30 to £23.30, but it is only in the last few years that pension increases have outstripped the rise in average earnings. A major landmark in the State provision of pensions was the passage on to the statute book in 1978 of an earnings related scheme for pensioners. The impact of this legislation will mean that a person on average earnings retiring in 1998 will get not far short of a half-pay pension.

During the 1950s and early 1960s there was also a growth in the number of workers in occupational pension schemes. In 1953, six million employees were in some sort of pension scheme related to their employment. By 1963, this had increased to eleven million (out of twenty-three million employees). From then the numbers in such schemes rose only slightly, totalling eleven and a half million in 1975. Between 1963 and 1975 the real value of occupational pensions remained virtually unchanged.

One of the key problems for unions is to preserve the real value of a worker's pension from the ravages of inflation. Only a few groups of workers have managed to achieve this. Since 1971, civil servants and other public services have had their pensions inflation-proofed after retirement. The nationalized industries have followed suit. The private sector has not.

By now three things should be obvious about your standard of living.

- You have never been guaranteed an adequate standard of living.
- We have all had to struggle since 1945 to improve, and latterly maintain, our living standards.
- The role of your trade union is vital in both defending and improving your standard of living.

Where does our standard of living come from?

Trade unionists' main concern is with the real factors in the economy such as growth and living standards.
(TUC Economic Review, 1977)

Economic growth

Our standard of living comes from economic growth. In Britain's mixed economy this means growth in both private and public enterprise. Unions in the private and public sector bargain for a share of this growth in the form of increased wages, holidays and pensions.

When Rab Butler, a minister in the Conservative Government of 1954, promised to double living standards in twenty-five years, he did so in the expectation of unparalleled growth and prosperity. History has proved him to be in part correct. Since the war the average growth rate of the British economy has been about 2½ per cent per annum. This is higher than at any other comparable period this century. Moreover, the rate of growth has remained fairly constant and up to 1973 there had only been two years of actual decline, 1952 and 1958. So, judged by its own historical standards, the economic performance of this country between 1945 and 1970 was pretty good. Unemployment was kept fairly low and the productivity of those employed rose annually by around 2 per cent in the early 1950s and around 3 per cent in the early 1970s.

Yet, during this same period, we slipped from being members of a comparatively high paid to a relatively low paid work-force. What went wrong?

Decline in manufacturing

The truth is that this country's economic performance appears in a different light when set against that of other industrial countries, most of which have higher growth rates. The result was that Britain's share of world trade in manufactured goods fell in every year from 1950 to 1973, with only one exception, 1971; at the beginning of the period this share was 25 per cent, by 1973 it was down to 9.5 per cent. Although the output of the manufacturing sector grew at a rate of 2.4 per cent each year between 1957 and 1977, it did little to offset the loss of competitiveness of British industry in world markets.

Two indicators, the collapse of the rate of profit and investment, demonstrate the decline of manufacturing industry. In the early 1950s international competition was weak; increased money wages won by trade unions could easily be passed on in the form of higher prices. As the climate of international competition stiffened in the middle and late 1960s this became more difficult to achieve. The rate of profit in manufacturing fell from about 12 per cent in the early sixties to some 4 per cent in the late seventies. Manufacturers were often forced to sell at prices below the actual cost of production. During the same period between 1960–64 and 1969–73, the share of investment in manufacturing industry fell from 23.8 per cent of all investment and likewise the share of manufacturing employment fell from 33.3 per cent to 31.9 per cent.

So, while workers in manufacturing lost their jobs, those with capital to invest turned their backs on Britain's declining industrial base. Investment was more likely to have financed another form of growth, in company mergers. It is estimated that by 1968 the twenty-eight largest companies in this country owned at least 40 per cent of the total assets of all manufacturing companies. There were other diversions too, like the growing property boom and investment in global manufacturing processes involving the labour of the developing countries.

Public sector growth

Growth also took place in the public sector. In the latter half of the 1950s and early 1960s public expenditure was a relatively stable proportion of total output. The years since the early 1960s have been characterized by a rapid growth. In 1960, public expenditure accounted for 36.5 per cent of Britain's national product; by 1977 this figure had reached 52.8 per cent. We saw in Chapter three how much of this expenditure was related to real needs. For example, public expenditure on education increased about three-and-a-half times between 1957 and 1977. Much of the cost of this increased expenditure fell on workers as less and less tax was deducted from the profit of companies. In 1950, the average manual worker and his family paid very little tax; in 1960, he paid only 8 per cent and by 1970 this figure had reached 18 per cent of his wage. Between 1966 and 1971 income tax (taken from wages) rose two and a half times as fast as corporation tax (taken from profits).

The recent failure of the post-war economy to generate sufficient growth has had a marked impact on our standard of living. Working class people have borne the full weight of successive crises, from the balance of payments deficits in the sixties, through the inflationary seventies, to the oil-rich eighties. On each occasion it is they who have been blamed for seeking to improve their standard of living. Increased taxation, prices, income restraint and more recently mass unemployment have been used to check our expectations of better living standards. Surprisingly, even under these extreme pressures, the unions have tried to move forward.

How have trade unions tried to control our living standards?

We can now see that many different things influence our standard of living – our own expectations, wages, the level of taxation, education, changes in government policy – all of which are interconnected. If trade unions are to respond adequately to our demands for real improvements in our living standards, they have to adopt methods of working that can embrace all of these complex issues. Since 1945, the unions have used a combination of three methods, collective bargaining, legislation and increasing public expenditure, in an effort to improve our standard of living. Behind each of these methods is an attempt to exert a measure of control over the factors which affect living standards. By control, we mean the ability of the unions to promote their own objectives, as well as their power to resist undesirable ones. For example, you want a substantial wage increase, which your employer is prepared to concede, but only in return for a reduction in the number of people employed. In Chapter three we saw how this struggle for control brings clashes with governments and within the unions themselves.

Let's take a look at the way in which the unions have tried to control the standard of living of some groups of workers.

Control over earnings – the engineering workers

We saw in Chapter two how, in the early sixties, the significance of national bargaining, particularly in engineering, diminished as a result of shop-floor pressure and employers responding to a shortage of workers. Unions at local level were able to exert pressure on individual employers for an increase in their living standards. This pressure had two results, it enabled workers to push up their own earnings and exact a high degree of job control. Local agreements on wages meant that rises in actual earnings tended to exceed rises in nationally agreed rates. In the sixteen years from 1949 to 1965 average earnings increased by 163 per cent against an increase of 129 per cent in wage rates. This process became known as wage drift.

In engineering the struggle over workers' living standards found its way on to the shop-floor where in many respects unions were at their strongest. The engineering industry in Coventry presents us with a good illustration of why and how this came about. In the 1960s the great majority of Coventry's production workers were paid by piece-work.

Shop-stewards were able to negotiate about piece-work prices for small groups of workers. This system not only strengthened union control but also provided sufficient wage drift for them not to require any formal pay negotiations. Local managements soon became disenchanted with this process and responded by introducing payment systems which had little or no incentive element. These forms of payment became known collectively as measured daywork. Management was prepared to buy-off union control. By the end of 1973, the shift from piece-work to job evaluated pay structures was well under way in many of the Coventry factories. Control passed from workgroup bargaining to plant-wide bargaining, where shop-stewards' committees rather than individual stewards did the negotiating.

Control over earnings did not stop in a single factory, it spread to cover a whole industry. In the car industry this was achieved through claims for equal payment, or parity, among carworkers. During the 1960s the earnings of Ford workers fell behind those of piece-workers in the Midland car firms. This situation was tolerated until the end of the decade when the demand for parity was widely voiced. Pressure arose initially at shop-floor level, but wage relativities were documented in detail in an official claim submitted at the end of 1970. That claim marked the beginning of a campaign for parity with Midland carworkers, which was backed by industrial action, and over a two-year period served to narrow the inter-company differentials considerably. During the 1970s the position was therefore reversed, and the fortunes of carworkers in the Midlands, mainly employed by British Leyland, suffered a grave decline. Between 1970 and 1978 their average earnings fell by 13.8 per cent to a position well below the average for the industry. This was in marked contrast to the South East, and the major Ford factories, where pay was still well above the national average.

Local bargainers saw the effectiveness of workplace organization, and parity with other groups of workers as a key concern in their struggle to control earnings. Unions at national level have adapted their own organization to accommodate this pressure from below. They have been so successful that in the 1970s the trend was reversed and attempts were made to consolidate improvements gained at the workplace into national agreements.

Bargaining strength and control – the miners

Not all workers have benefited from their union's ability to transfer negotiations to the place of work. Control of living standards has sometimes been more effective when unions have established a national platform on which to argue their case. The miners were one group of workers, who in the post-war decades, found that 'unity is strength'. Up until the mid-1960s most negotiations in mining were conducted at pit level where piece-work predominated. This form of local bargaining only satisfied the demands of particular workgroups, setting miner against miner and pit against pit. Conflict over wages was frequent, but strikes were localised.

In 1966 the NUM signed the Power Loading Agreement which transferred most face-workers from piece-work to day work on rates of pay settled in industry-wide negotiations. Although strikes fell off, discontent was mounting about the decline in the miners' standard of living. In 1957 miners' earnings were 125 per cent of manufacturing earnings; by 1970 they had dropped to 97 per cent. The net result was that miners dropped from third to twelfth place in the earnings league. The move towards national bargaining had acted as a unifying force bringing together the otherwise independent regions into a single union. This unity was of major importance in the eventful strikes of 1972 and 1974. This new found strength enabled the miners to go some way to restoring their earnings to their previous level.

Once again the employers hit back. Towards the close of the seventies the employers reintroduced the idea of pit-based productivity schemes. In December 1977, after much internal wrangling, the executive committee of the NUM voted to allow areas to introduce incentive payments. The militant coalfields of Kent, South Wales, Scotland and Yorkshire failed in their attempt to obtain a court injunction restraining the executive from implementing this decision. The introduction of productivity schemes has started to break-down the cohesion which served the miners so well.

The example of the miners is perhaps exceptional in that the relative position of most occupations in the earnings league has remained virtually unchanged since 1945. But for the miners and other groups like gas workers, petrol-tanker drivers and dockers in the larger ports, the control they have exercised through bargaining has been short-lived.

Organization and control – the case of workers in the public sector

In Chapter three we noted that there is a real difference in the numerical strength of trade unions in the public and private sectors. In the public sector eight out of ten workers were organized compared to five out of ten in private manu-facturing industry. Does this strength in numbers automati-cally mean a greater control over living standards? If we look at pay, the issue is in some doubt.

The graph in Figure 9 shows how the differential between private and public sector earnings appears to have been steadily narrowing since the early 1970s. Up until the end of the 1960s pay for private sector manual workers was gen-erally above that of their public sector counterparts; the line on the graph is above the 100 per cent mark. The change in the 1970s, which was especially sharp between 1974–75, re-sulted in a movement in favour of the public sector of some sixteen percentage points between October 1969 and April 1975 (follow the path of the dotted line on the graph). By 1976 this improvement had meant that the relative pay of manual workers was more than 10 per cent higher than it had been in the 1950s and 1960s. It is perhaps better ex-plained like this:

On average a manual worker in the car industry must now work the same (thirty minutes) as in 1970 to earn enough to buy a gallon of petrol; for the manual worker in local government the time has fallen from 48 to 38 minutes.
A. B. Atkinson, *New Society*, April 1979

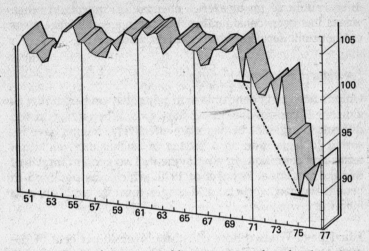

Figure 9 Ratio of private to public sector manual workers' earnings.
Source: J. Dean, 'Public and Private Sector Manual Workers' Pay 1970–77', National Institute Economic Review No. 82, 1977.

The growing militancy of public service workers and the effects of one particular incomes policy, in 1975–6, which allowed a flat rate increase, accounted for this change. In any event, these gains proved to be short-lived. Table 6 shows that since 1975, public sector workers have recorded smaller increases in earnings than private sector workers.

Table 6 Percentage increases in average earnings April 1975–78

	Manual men	Non-manual men	All men	Manual women	Non-manual women	All women
Public sector	39.8	41.9	42.3	45.6	43.7	43.5
Private sector	47.2	51.1	49.2	58.1	55.9	57.0

Source: *Department of Employment Gazette* December 1977, New Earnings Survey Part A 1978.

A high degree of unionization is no guarantee of a higher living standard. In the last fifteen years, the efforts of unions

89

in the public sector to exert a measure of control over their wages has been considerable. But there are still large areas of the public services which are low paid.

Legislation as a form of control

Unions have not been content to rely solely on bargaining as a means of control over living standards. When it has proved difficult to organize or negotiate effectively, unions have resorted to legislation as a means of establishing minimum terms and conditions of employment. Two good examples of this are the Equal Pay Act of 1970, which was designed to benefit women workers, and wages councils established to help the low paid.

Equal pay Women now constitute over 40 per cent of the work-force. The majority of women workers are in non-manual jobs (one third are in clerical occupations) and are highly concentrated in services (by 1978 over 58 per cent were employed in the three main service areas: distributive trades, education/health services and miscellaneous services – catering, etc.). On average they earn considerably less than men, even after making allowances for the fact that they work on average shorter hours and do less overtime.

As Figure 10 shows, the gap between male and female earnings has narrowed in recent years. There are two factors which accounted for this change. The impact of the 1970 Equal Pay Act, the provisions of which came fully into force at the end of 1975. The movement of women's pay in the short-run was strongly influenced by this legislation and the fact that moves towards equal pay were generally exempted from statutory pay limits up until the end of 1975. The other reason for progress on this issue was that during the 1970s women were becoming unionized, by 1978 they formed 28.7 per cent of TUC membership. This undoubtedly increased the level of activity on equal pay. Since 1977, progress towards equality, just in terms of pay, has been halted and even declined to the 1975 level. The gains made by legislative means have been temporary. They were eroded by other

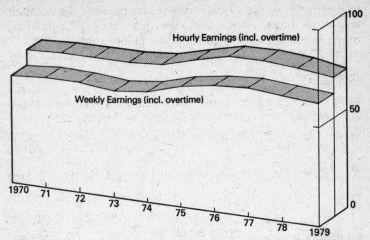

Figure 10 Average female earnings as a percentage of average male earnings

Source: New Earnings Survey. Cited in *Low Pay Report No. 2: Low Pay Policies* Clive Playford, Low Pay Unit, October 1980.

groups of workers who have resisted the pressure towards equality by seeking to maintain differentials.

'At SU,' said Griffiths, a local AUEW official, 'women production workers are earning £56 per week. The toolroom workers are on £60.30. Their status and pride, with their income, has taken a hefty knock in recent years.'

(The dispute at SU Carburettor, Birmingham 1976 – *New Society* April 1976.

Low pay Both the TUC and its individual affiliates have believed for most of the last fifty years that the proper way to deal with low pay was for trade unions to attack it through collective bargaining. The TUC defines low pay as any wage below two-thirds of the average adult male pay. The practice has been to establish minimum targets for bargainers to achieve, in 1968 it was £15 which had doubled to £30 by 1975. Despite this commitment, which has been bolstered by the fair wages law, the Equal Pay Act, wages councils and successive incomes policies, the relative earnings of the low paid are now no higher than they were before the war. Table 7 opposite shows evidence of the extent of low pay among male and female workers.

It shows that in the 1970s the only inroad has been made by women workers whose unsteady progress towards equal pay has removed a number from the low paid category.

- It is obvious from the above that six out of ten women workers are low paid.
- Manual workers, particularly in the public services, are low earners.
- The elderly and young are disproportionately represented amongst the low paid. The figures in the table, excluding overtime, would probably double if the young and part-time workers were included. In 1977 92.6 per cent of the under eighteens and 50.6 per cent of the eighteen to twenty-year-olds were classed as low paid.
- Low earners are concentrated among particular occupations, farming, selling and distribution, but few occupational groups are without some low earners.

There are a number of obstacles in the way of trade union attempts to aid the lower paid. The first is the absence of collective bargaining. The TUC are right to assert that an extension of bargaining would probably reduce the incidence of low pay. The relationship between collective bargaining and low pay can be seen from Table 8.

Table 8 Pay levels and collective bargaining

Weekly earnings distribution position	Percentage not covered by collective agreements	
	men	women
top two-thirds	14	22
bottom one-third	25	45

Source: *New Society*, October 1980.

This refers to full-time adult manual workers in 1973. A worker in the bottom third of the earnings league is twice as

Table 7 Low paid workers* Numbers and percentages, 1970–79 (April each year)

	Including overtime				Excluding overtime			
	Men		Women		Men		Women	
	No	%	No	%	No	%	No	%
1970	1.1m	10.1	3.4m	70.8	–	–	–	–
1971	1.2m	10.8	3.4m	69.4	–	–	–	–
1972	1.1m	9.9	3.4m	68.0	2.1m	18.9	3.4m	68.0
1973	1.3m	11.8	3.6m	72.0	2.4m	21.8	3.7m	74.0
1974	1.0m	9.7	3.3m	66.0	2.0m	18.7	3.5m	70.0
1975	1.0m	9.7	2.8m	59.6	1.5m	14.6	2.9m	61.7
1976	1.0m	9.8	2.4m	51.1	1.5m	16.7	2.8m	60.0
1977	0.9m	9.0	2.5m	53.0	1.4m	14.0	2.6m	55.0
1978	1.0m	9.9	2.6m	56.5	1.7m	16.8	2.7m	58.7
1979	1.0m	10.1	2.7m	58.7	1.7m	17.2	2.8m	60.9

Source: Low Pay Policies, Clive Playford, op. cit.

*The low paid are defined here as in other Low Pay Unit publications, as those full-time workers who earn less than two thirds of average (median) male earnings (for an explanation of this definition see 'Low Pay in the 80s', Low Pay Unit Bulletin No 30, December 1979.)

likely not to be covered by a collective bargaining agreement as a worker in the top two thirds. A recent estimate showed that these same workers could expect earnings which were roughly a fifth or more higher if they were employed in an industry or occupation which was 100 per cent covered by collective bargaining. A second obstacle is the restraints imposed on negotiations by incomes policies and wage councils; both of which were supposedly designed to help the low paid. But they have failed. The industries covered by the thirty-four wage councils, which established the minimum pay of some 2.75 million low paid workers, continue to pay subsistence wage and trade union organization in such sectors remains poor. A third obstacle placed in the way of unions is the fiscal (tax) policy of governments. Lower-paid workers have found that increased government deductions from wages have often eroded the benefits of any pay award.

The final obstacle is the attitude of many unions to the lower paid. Only NUPE, the public service union, with over half its membership in the lowest income groups, has actively campaigned for a national minimum wage. Generally support for the lower paid, as in the case of women, is not allowed to disturb occupational differentials.

We have looked briefly at how successful unions have been in trying to control a major part of our standard of living, namely our pay. We saw how some groups have moved up and down the economic ladder; some gaining and some losing; and how the overall pattern was little altered. It will come as no surprise to learn that the general distribution of earnings has changed relatively little in the post-war years. In 1959, the top 10 per cent of the population had 25 per cent of earnings after tax and the bottom 50 per cent also shared 25 per cent. By 1976 the top 10 per cent received a slightly smaller proportion, 22½ per cent, and the bottom 50 per cent had increased their share to 27½ per cent. Figures like these do not represent the significant changes that have taken place as unions have tried to improve living standards. Remember in the 1920s unions struggled to resist savage wage cuts. Viewed in this light, the extension of union control represents a genuine challenge to market forces, which today are still demanding wage cuts rather than increases.

Under these circumstances is it reasonable to expect the unions, on their own, to resolve the basic problems of low pay? This one is hard to answer. The examples of control we have looked at suggest that the existing methods of collective bargaining backed up by legislation, will not resolve the problem. Indeed, each of the groups we looked at revealed something about the weaknesses of bargaining as an effective form of control over living standards.

● The engineers, showed how often bargaining is extremely narrow and defensive.
● The miners, showed how even today the so-called change in the balance of bargaining power to the advantage of organized workers can be exaggerated.
● The public employees, showed how even 100 per cent membership would not guarantee favourable results from bargaining.
● Women workers, showed how bargaining reflects the social and political status quo, it does not challenge the existing reward structure.
● The low paid, showed how bargaining over control takes place in a rigid occupational framework, which supports the division of worker from worker.

In themselves these are not answers, but they do suggest some possible explanations. They suggest why powerful groups, like the miners, have been unable to help the low-paid garment worker, or why the engineering unions have done so little to promote equality. An understanding of these problems is important if the union movement is to progress in the next twenty years.

Why have unions experienced difficulty in maintaining our standard of living?

In the previous pages we have already seen two possible answers to this question, a lack of economic growth or a weakness in trade union methods. In this section we will suggest a third, the strength of the opposition unions have faced. The 'opposition' has been provided by employers and governments, whose economic priorities have seldom co-incided with those of unions when it came to improving the standard of living.

The challenge of the employers

Unions and employers have always opposed each other. Employers' attempts to restrain costs and improve efficiency have often clashed head on with the traditional trade union objectives of raising their members' wages and protecting their jobs. As we have seen in an earlier section the return to full employment in the 1950s the spread of workplace bargaining, linked initially to piece-work, strengthened the control which small work-groups and their shop-stewards had over production and wages. It was the falling rate of company profitability which finally prompted employers through their management, to devise a counterattack. Quite simply, employers began looking for a pay system that would once again subordinate the pay structure to managerial control. Any major development of this kind had to achieve three objectives:

- regain control of pay;
- resolve the problem of labour shortage by making skilled workers more flexible;
- draw the sting of the shop-stewards by involving them in discussions over changes in working practice.

In this section we take a brief look at these attempts to reassert managerial control.

Our starting point must be the phase of productivity bargaining which took place during the 1960s. The term productivity bargain has come to mean many things, but is basically:

. . . an agreement in which advantages of one kind or another such as higher wages or increased leisure are given to workers in return for agreement on their part to accept changes in working practice

or in methods or in organization which will lead to more efficient working.
Donovan Commission 1967 Research Paper No. 4.

Workers had to weigh up the advantages against the changes in working practices. The first indication that such agreements were being entered into came from the oil industry. Between 1960 and 1968 the Esso Company reached a series of 'comprehensive plant agreements' at its Fawley refinery which were to establish the pattern for that industry and many others. This was the first productivity package deal in which large pay increases (40 per cent over two years) were negotiated in return for specified changes in working practices. The pay increases were not only necessary to get agreement for the changes in working practices but also to compensate the workers for the drastic, although phased, reduction in overtime working. The package included assurances that there would be no redundancies and allowed for a reduction of the working week by two hours in return for the withdrawal of non-productive time allowances amounting to three and a half hours per week.

The pattern was set and repeated elsewhere, at the company level in British Oxygen (1966) and Courtaulds (1968) and on an industry-wide basis in chemicals. The agreements differed widely in their scope but the sorts of issues bargained about were similar:

● the removal of excessive overtime, increased flexibility in the use of labour among skilled trades and between skilled and less skilled workers;
● changes in manning levels;
● the cutting out of non-work time and reductions in the number of workers employed.

In return, unions anticipated a higher standard of living in the form of higher earnings, increased holidays and sick pay, shorter hours and better fringe benefits. In 1966, just over half a million workers were covered by productivity agreements. By the end of 1969 it was claimed that over 3500 separate agreements covering six million workers (one in four of the labour force) had been negotiated. This sudden upsurge of interest in productivity conveniently coincided with attempts by government to introduce incomes policy.

It became deliberate government policy, particularly during the years of the Labour administration between 1964 and 1970, to advocate the negotiation of productivity agreements within the framework of successive prices and incomes policies. Much of this was foreshadowed in an earlier, 1962, White Paper from the then Conservative Government. They believed that incomes needed to be kept in line with the growth in national productivity and wage increases could only be justified on certain grounds.

There may, however, be cases in which an increase could be justified as part of an agreement under which those concerned made a direct contribution, by accepting more exacting work, or more onerous conditions, or by a renunciation of restrictive practices, to an increase of productivity and a reduction of costs.'

White Paper, Incomes policy: the next step, February 1962.

The appointment of the National Board for Prices and Incomes in 1965 marked a major increase in State involvement in pay determination. Through this agency the government set out to establish productivity as the major criterion for wage negotiations. In a short period of time, productivity deals passed from being an attempt by management to regain control to an arm of government policy. Thereafter, the initiative was taken up by the unions themselves as the only means of securing high wage increases above the ceilings and norms imposed by incomes policies. When the initiative passed to shop-floor bargainers agreements came to concentrate far more on conventional wage claims. Many of the deals negotiated during this later period bore little resemblance to the Fawley prototype. On many occasions productivity bargaining was little different to ordinary bargaining between unions and employers, with perhaps one notable exception – the issue of jobs.

In the early 1960s, the Steel Company of Wales decided that there should be no more traditional bargaining. They opted for productivity bargaining in an attempt to prevent the unions using the cost of living, company profitability and parity as arguments in securing wage increases. The company's strategy was to divide the unions, 'persuading one group of unions to finance the deal (through job loss and reductions in earnings) and another group to give up certain jobs'. The unions' main problem, recalled one commentator, 'will be convincing those declared redundant that they could move to some more highly paid job'. (E. Owen Smith, *Productivity Bargaining*, Pan 1971.) In the event large numbers of workers lost their jobs.

It was the narrowness of productivity as a basis for wage claims and the resultant job loss, which forced unions to turn away from productivity bargaining in the early 1970s. The experience was similar in the public sector where the application of productivity bargaining to particular services, like refuse collection and hospitals, meant that gains could only come from reduced manpower. In deteriorating economic circumstances, with rising unemployment and high levels of inflation, productivity bargaining became a less acceptable means of conducting pay negotiations. In June 1971, for instance, the AEUW announced that it had decided not to sign any more productivity deals that might increase unemployment. In the same year the TUC, in their Economic Review, warned of the dangers of relying on productivity as the sole criterion for wage increases.

. . . unless the Government is prepared to allow economic expansion, the same output is being shared out amongst fewer men as productivity rises. This will force unions to refuse cooperation in raising productivity.

TUC Economic Review 1971.

In the mid-1970s, successive managements abandoned incentive payment systems which they had failed to control and resorted to measured daywork. Cash incentives were replaced by a general increase in supervision.

. . . since MDW replaced piece-work the factory has gone supervision crazy. The ratio of foremen to production workers has gone down from 60 to 1 to 18 to 1.

Cliff Moss, Senior Chairman Stewards, Cowley, quoted in *New Society*, October 1977.

Towards the end of the 1970s, however, productivity bargaining was set to make a comeback. The ingredients were the same. An initiative from the employers was given added impetus by the constraints of a new round of pay policies. On this occasion the employers were anxious to introduce new technology. Flexibility and new working practices have now come to mean more productivity with machines rather than workers, a fact which is already apparent to many print workers, car workers and post-office engineers. We return to this theme of the impact of technological change upon living standards in the final chapter.

Employers have tried three major strategies to control the demands of workers. Firstly, as we have already seen they resorted to passing increased costs on to their workers, in the form of increased prices. Secondly, in order to encourage greater output they have tried new forms of wage bargaining. The 1960s version of productivity bargaining which was aimed at the shop-floor workers was extended to job evaluation in the 1970s and covered staff employees as well. Finally, the growth in the size and scale of multinational enterprises coupled with the adoption of new advances in technology have allowed employers greater freedom to invest where labour is cheapest. A consequence of this has been a reduction in the numbers employed, through redundancies and unemployment. The employers' challenge to our living standards is clear. In the post-war years they have tried to play-off our demands for high pay against attempts by unions to exert a measure of job control. The choice between raising money wages or increased unemployment is not a real choice for any of us.

The State and living standards

In Chapter three we showed how State intervention has become a major feature of industrial relations in the last thirty years. Governments, with their concern about incomes and their steady expansion of responsibilities as an employer, have been reluctant to allow unions and management to bargain freely. In this section we look at the effects of two forms of government intervention, incomes policy and the social wage, on our standards of living.

Politicians in the early 1950s were prepared to express concern at the level of wage settlements. Ten years later, those politicans were establishing various kinds of machinery to try to influence the level of pay settlements. This process, whereby government attempted to 'alter the national level of wages and salaries, or to alter the rate at which they change' has become known as incomes policy (H. A. Clegg, *The System of Industrial Relations in Great Britain* Blackwell, 1972). After 1961 both major political parties promised a higher rate of economic growth. Both emphasized the problem of wage inflation and considered the rate of wage increases produced by collective bargaining since 1945 threatened the maintenance of full employment. The Governments of Wilson, Heath and Callaghan were to seek wage restraint and interfere with, and at times prevent, collective bargaining taking place. These policies presented a serious challenge to the ability of unions to exercise their power to improve members' living standards.

While successive governments may have had similar aims in the field of wage bargaining they have gone about it very differently. For a start they have used a variety of institutional arrangements to implement policies. Another important difference between the policies was whether they were voluntary or compulsory. The policies operated by the Conservatives in the early 1960s were little more than appeals by government ministers for restraint in wage bargaining. The compulsory policy of 1966–7, for example, was based upon a wage freeze. In contrast the policy of 1974 linked wage increases to movements in prices through threshold agreements. The phase of incomes policy between 1975 and 1979 represented an unprecedented period of voluntary control over wages. A further important distinction between the various incomes policies was the extent of the allowances for 'special factors' such as productivity, low pay or labour mobility.

It is difficult to describe the range of policies adopted and even harder to assess the union response. The attitude of the

101

TUC, individual union leaders and their membership has changed with each phase of policy. There were three main phases of incomes policy since 1964. The unions were involved in the 1964–70 Labour Government's policies mainly through their Incomes Policy Committee. This committee was established by the TUC in October 1965 to vet the claims of its members, largely in order to forestall the introduction of statutory powers which was being threatened by the Labour Government. This plan succeeded for just ten months. The TUC and all affiliated unions adopted a policy of non-cooperation with the Conservative Government's policies in 1972–4. For the most recent period of the 'social contract' between 1975–9 they have played a key role, both in suggesting what the policy should be, implementing it and finally bringing it to an end. In any event, unions have only been allowed by their members to countenance short periods of income restraint. Furthermore, unions have insisted on governments pursuing price controls and certain other social and economic objectives in return for this limited support.

Workers themselves have provided the main opposition to incomes policy. It was shop-floor pressure in 1950, 1968, 1977 and 1979 which brought about changes in policy or a return to free collective bargaining. There are a number of reasons why workers have felt aggrieved about wage restraint:

● Firstly, incomes policy hasn't applied to everyone. For a start nearly two million workers are self-employed. Other groups such as barristers and solicitors have ignored the successive policies and raised their fees to suit their tastes. Higher paid employees have got round pay policies through promotions, job changes and the evasion of limits.

● Pay policies since 1970 have done little to narrow the differential between the highest and lowest paid. Progress for the low paid has often been a major determinant of the support of large unions like the TGWU and the GMWU, both of whom have large numbers of low earners amongst their membership. The largest reduction of differentials during that period was between June 1974 and June 1975, an era of free collective bargaining.

● There is little evidence that dividend or price controls have been applied with the same zest as the control on wages.

● Finally, tax changes have made a nonsense of the concept of incomes control. In the period of incomes policy between July 1975 and October 1977 a person earning £25,000 had income tax changes worth an extra £7226, equivalent to a pay rise of 28.9 per cent. A person earning £1500 would have gained in his pocket an extra £103, equivalent to only 6.9 per cent

(Ruskin Trade Union Research Unit, Technical Note 39.)

Most workers and their stewards supported formal incomes policy as an emergency measure to be adopted in special circumstances. In the periods after incomes policy they swiftly acted to restore earnings to their previous level.

Figure 11 shows how wage increases in the period immediately following the ending of policies were higher than during the period of operation of policies. Workers have managed to regain what was lost during incomes policy, but that was all.

When these policies failed, such as in 1968, both the Conservative opposition and the Labour Government shifted their strategy towards a reform of industrial relations law. By 1972, the Conservative Government had imposed a ceiling on public sector wage claims. This sparked off a wave of conflicts greater than, and occurring simultaneously with, those over the Industrial Relations Act. Even the period of positive labour legislation embarked upon by the Wilson Government between February 1974 and June 1975 was ultimately insufficient to persuade organized workers to endure a prolonged period of income restraint. In comparison with incomes policy, legal reform has had little impact upon workers' standards of living.

The other strategy governments have adopted for controlling workers' living standards is related to the issue of public expenditure. They have either cut back the pay or jobs of public sector workers or reduced the level of expenditure on

103

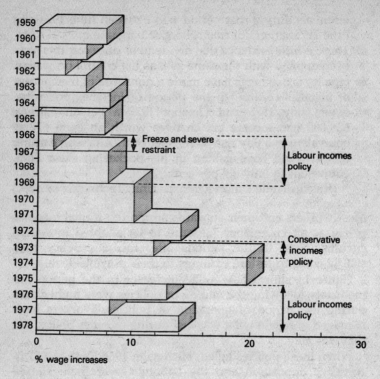

Figure 11 Changes in average earnings 1959–78.

Source: *The Reform of the Wage Bargaining System* F. Blackaby,
National Institute Economic Review No. 85, 1978.

production (steel, coal, etc.) and services (education, health, etc.). In the case of late 1970s and early 1980s both policies have been pursued with vigour, by first a Labour and then Conservative administration. To trade unions this strategy has become known as an attack on 'the social wage'. This wage, which is provided by government as distinct from the wage paid by employers, has played an increasingly significant role in determining our living standards.

The phrase is used to refer to the average benefit received by the population from a wide variety of items of public expenditure. This concept of the social wage was first extensively marketed by government spokesmen during 1975 to counter growing discontent at the level of wage taxation. 'The taxman,' explained Barbara Castle as Social Services Secretary, 'is the Robin Hood of our time taking from those who can afford it the means whereby we can pay every worker the wage that really matters, the social wage.' It has thereafter been a concept that politicians and the press have flaunted before us whenever it can be interpreted as contributing to improved living standards. It is conveniently discarded whenever the results are unfavourable. The definition of the social wage is itself a problem and there is a good deal of disagreement about which categories of public expenditure should, or should not, be included. Table 9 shows an increase in the social wage. Much of the increase is accounted for by the rise in public expenditure on the unemployed. It is also debatable whether items like defence expenditure should be included. Between 1973–4 and 1974–5 there was a significant increase of just over £3 a week in the 'real' value of the social wage (column 3).

Table 9 The social wage (official estimates)

Financial year	1 Per week	2 As percentage of average earnings of adult male workers	3 Real value at 1978 survey prices
	£	%	£
1973–4	13.90	34.0	28.10
1974–5	18.70	38.5	31.35
1975–6	23.50	39.4	31.63
1976–7	26.40	39.4	31.13
1977–8	28.60	39.2	30.29
1978–9	31.50	37.7	31.50

Published in *Federation News* Vol. 29 No. 4 October 1979 from a paper produced by the Trade Union Research Unit, Oxford.

Thus both as a proportion of average earnings and in real

terms there was a marked increase in the value of the social wage shortly after the last Labour government was elected. Between 1977–8 and 1978–9 the 'real' value of the social wage increased whereas as a proportion of average earnings it decreased. This shows that for the first time in a few years there had been an improvement in gross pay. The value of the social wage is determined by the quality of the services provided which the above table doesn't measure. Any cuts in public expenditure will seriously unde.mine the living standards of a major part of the working population.

Unions have had a difficult time convincing workers that the social wage is a by-product of collective bargaining. Firstly, there is the obvious fact that not everyone benefits to the same extent from public expenditure. It is not easy to convince all workers that their standard of living is increased by government expenditure. Some groups, those with children, the low paid and the unemployed, will in part rely upon the social wage for their income. Secondly, in certain instances, such as in the case of the low paid, a wage increase negotiated by unions could lead to a loss of income from the social wage, which in the end leaves them worse off. Thirdly, they see their living standards being dependent upon private decisions about what they should or should not spend from their take-home pay. Finally, unions themselves obviously cannot claim to have control over the social wage.

In the post-war period successive governments, both Conservative and Labour, have adopted one of three strategies to control union demands. They have either allowed unemployment or inflation to rise, or they have resorted to specific measures to limit the effectiveness of collective bargaining. On occasions, such as today, they have combined these various strategies.

Is there any conflict over living standards?

In this chapter we have shown how unions faced continuous pressure from their members to increase living standards. They had to achieve this in spite of considerable opposition from employers and governments. Conflict was not only likely, but inevitable. In this final section we consider how the fight for living standards has resulted in open conflict between groups of workers and their employers.

In the immediate post-war years, the days lost through strikes seldom rose above three million. Between 1944 and 1954 only 44.4 per cent of strikes were about pay. Less than half the working days lost were due to strikes about wages. In 1957, the year of a major confrontation in the engineering industry, 8.4 million days were lost, and the prolonged period of relative industrial calm which had started in the 1920s came to an end. During the upsurge in conflict between 1957 and 1962 the miners, dockers, car workers and building workers were to the fore.

Between 1960 and 1966 the annual average number of wage disputes was 1150 and approximately forty-eight out of every

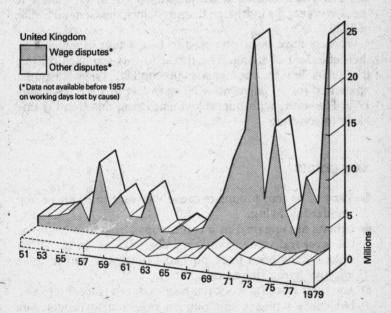

Figure 12 Industrial disputes: working days lost, by cause, 1951–77

Source: Social Trends, No. 11, Central Statistical Office, 1981.

hundred stoppages were over wage issues. Between 1967 and 1974 the annual average was 1560, with fifty-six out of every hundred disputes being about wages. In the period between 1967 and 1974 there has been an increase in absolute and proportionate terms in the number of strikes about all wage issues. There are two factors which explain this increase, unrest over incomes policy and the growth of militancy in the public sector. All manual workers became involved in the wave of strikes between 1968 and 1972, unrest was not just confined to four or five industries. The main thrust behind these disputes was an aggressive demand for more money. The increase of official strikes in the public sector has added to the length of and numbers of workers involved in strikes about demands for wage increases. In 1979, the strike of engineering workers, again over pay, meant that sixteen million days were lost in just one major dispute. The 29.1 million working days lost in 1979 made it the worst year for industrial disputes since the General Strike of 1926.

Workers have been prepared to take action in support of their standard of living. The threat to this standard during the 1970s led to an increase in conflict. Wage disputes accounted for 90 per cent of all days lost in 1972, 1974 and 1979. However, with unemployment rising this trend is unlikely to continue.

Key points

- Most of us join unions because we want to improve our standard of living.
- Unions are engaged in a continuous struggle to improve the level and value of their members wages. In the 1970s unions have been hard pushed to maintain rather than improve living standards.
- The basic working week has been reduced since the 1950s, but many workers still rely on overtime to provide an adequate wage.
- The protection of living standards during retirement is still

unsatisfactory for most groups of workers, particularly manual workers, but has improved since the war.

● Unions have attempted in different ways to exert some control over their members' living standards, using collective bargaining, protective legislation and demands for increased public expenditure to achieve this end.

● The overall distribution of pay and benefits has changed little during our period and the problems of low pay, especially amongst women workers, remain.

● Employers have resisted workers' demands for increased living standards by raising prices, adopting new forms of payment and bargaining, by resorting to new methods of production or investing abroad.

● The State has taken a more interventionist role in managing the economy and attempted to control workers' living standards via incomes policy, cuts in public expenditure and restrictive legislation.

● The level of industrial conflict over living standards has greatly increased since 1945, and this has involved many groups of workers new to trade unionism.

Discussion

● What goes to make up your standard of living?
● What do you think has happened to your standard of living in the last ten years?
● What action should unions take to both defend and improve our living standards in the future?

Further reading

It's difficult to recommend specific reading on the standard of living. Your union journal will probably give you an idea of agreements and progress in your industry.

For a more general view you could follow the same course we did. Firstly, look at monthly copies of *Labour Research* which can be ordered from Labour Research Department, 78 Blackfriars Road, London SE1 8HF. This is a useful publication written especially for trade unionists. Secondly your public library will doubtless contain copies of the journal *New Society* and the government annual statistics publication, *Social Trends*. Both contain periodic references to living standards.

Finally you could look for books which explain changes in the economy. The best one we have come across recently is called *The British Economic Disaster* by Andrew Glyn and John Harrison from Pluto Press. It is a good account of changes in the economy and can be fairly easily understood.

Chapter **five**

What has happened to our jobs?

This chapter examines jobs and looks at the following aspects:

- Are there enough jobs available for the people who want them?
- How secure are people's jobs?
- What sort of movement is there between jobs, both within and between workplaces?

We want to see how these three aspects have altered in the post war years. We shall begin from the assumption that there are two basic concerns when we look at this area:

- Firstly, what has been called the right to work; that is whether society can provide jobs for all the people who want to work.
- Secondly, we all desire a degree of job security; we don't want to be sacked and we don't want either to find that our job is constantly changing or that our place of work is always being altered.

The chapter will try, therefore, to examine how successful unions have been in achieving these objectives of job security and the right to work.

An overview of the period suggests that it has become increasingly difficult to achieve these aims. Since the war:

- Redundancy has become more and more frequent. In the late sixties and seventies there were between half a million and a million redundancies every year.
- There has been more and more mobility of labour (or flexibility of labour) so that the actual jobs people do have been subject to greater change.
- Unemployment has risen dramatically. The average level of unemployment in the fifties was around the 334,000 mark, in the sixties it had risen to 447,000. Throughout the seventies unemployment went up sharply, first to one million, then to two million, and then to two and a half million. All the signs are that it is continuing to rise and will do so indefinitely.

We will look at how and why this has happened and end with some questions about union policies in the eighties.

Worker 'resistance to change' in the fifties

In his history of the 1964–70 Labour Government, Harold Wilson recalls speaking to a May Day meeting of his constituents in the Merseyside town of Kirkby. His theme, a favoured one, was union resistance to change.

. . . I condemned the 'Maginot line' of outmoded defensive practices behind which so many industrial workers vainly tried to shelter. I said, 'The defensive work-spreading practices bred in the years of

depression, so far from defending full employment and wage standards, are the surest way of endangering them'.

H. Wilson *The Labour Government 1964–70* (Penguin)

Throughout the late fifties and early sixties, the trade unions
often found themselves blamed for the problems facing the
British economy. Thus their 'high wages' have been accused
of pricing British goods out of the market; or their strike
record has put off customers whose orders couldn't be met
on time. In the 1950s this theme of restrictive practices was
a favoured one. Organized workers were told that they
should abandon this type of attitude and adopt a more up-
to-date approach to their jobs. But what were these restrictive
practices and how did they affect the jobs that people did?
One of their most important aspects was a strict definition of
what a particular person's job consisted of; everyone had his
or her own job and couldn't just be moved around to suit
the employer's changing requirements. The origins lay with
the organization of skilled workers and their insistence:

- that particular jobs could only be done by members of
  their craft;
- that there should be a clear distinction between work done
  by skilled (or qualified) workers and that done by non-
  skilled workers – 'mates' or labourers.

This approach to jobs has been caricatured frequently, for
example 'only a skilled electrician is allowed to change a
plug' or 'it takes ten men to repair a simple machine break-
down because of the different skills involved'. It was also
criticized by many workers because it prevented people who
hadn't entered an apprenticeship after leaving school from
developing additional skills and earning more money. Some
groups of workers had an entirely different view. For instance, stewards at the huge Austin car factory in Birmingham argued:

'The attitude of the shop-steward organization is that we do not
operate restrictive practices. The practices that have been operated
and any which the management might wish to complain about now,
are, in point of fact, protective practices, very necessary in the
period of management's hostility to the unions. When we were in

113

a position to prevent the management abusing us, we abolished most of these protective practices. . .'
Evidence of the Austin Joint Shop-Stewards Committee to the Donovan Commission.

This relatively rigid approach to jobs and the division between jobs had certain advantages both for the aim of job security and the right to work.

- the insistence on a craftsman working with a mate made it easier to maintain safe standards of work;
- employers had to employ more workers in order to ensure that all the different kinds of job could be done;
- most workers preferred a degree of regularity in their job rather than being moved around a great deal.

This desire by workers to restrict the right of management to move them around the work place did not just apply to skilled workers. For instance, in the motor industry, although a lot of the divisions between skills were breaking down in the post war years, the unions usually imposed restrictions on management's right to move people around the factory. Similarly in other types of jobs. A teacher would be employed to teach in a particular school. A library assistant to work in a particular library. In both cases the local authority would have to employ additional staff, for example supply teachers, in order to cope with emergencies, such as a number of sicknesses in the same school. Because there was in many occupations in the fifties a shortage of labour, workers were often quite successful in maintaining these practices even though employers did not particularly like them. Increasingly, however, managements, often encouraged by the government, tried to find ways to break down these restrictions through increased flexibility and mobility of labour. Linked to this, too, was an increase in the rate of redundancy.

Redundancies

One of the greatest fears at the back of most of our minds is that of arriving at work one day and finding that our job has disappeared. This was true even in the fifties when overall there seemed to be enough jobs to go round. Every time there is a redundancy:

- some people, albeit a minority, will never get another job;
- some will spend a significant period looking for work;
- many will end up with jobs that they like less than the one from which they were made redundant, it may pay less well, it may be further from home, it may take them away from friends and former work mates, it may not be as satisfying or as interesting;
- a job disappears for the future generation.

All this happens in a period of 'full employment'. One industry which, as we saw in Chapter one lost a lot of jobs was the cotton industry. This industry was concentrated in the cotton towns of the north-west of England. In the six months between September 1959 and the end of March 1960 there was a massive programme of redundancies in the cotton industry with some of the mill towns being particularly hard hit:

Table 10

Town	Number of Redundancies
Bolton	3104
Blackburn	2022
Burnley	2383
Nelson	2416
Oldham	7711

Source: R. Naylor, 'Redundancy in Cotton'. *New Society*, March 1963.

Yet it is recorded that unemployment figures for the cotton towns showed no 'striking increase' during this period. What happened to the redundant mill-workers? Firstly a significant proportion retired from the labour force, this was particularly true of women, old people and partially disabled people. They did this for a variety of reasons. For example:

An unmarried weaver in her fifties had arthritis in her hip and could only move awkwardly and slowly. She had been able to run four Lancashire looms for the reduced hours which her former employer allowed her as an old company servant. She was physically unable to move around the greater number of looms in a modern set-up and she could not obtain the same concession in hours.

(quoted in R. Naylor op. cit.)

Many of those who 'disappeared' from the labour force never showed up on the unemployment statistics because they wouldn't or didn't register at the Labour Exchange. Those who got other jobs did not fare that well either. A survey was conducted of one of the main skilled male grades, the mule spinners. Of 1193 who were made redundant in Oldham, 934 got other jobs (two-thirds returning to the cotton industry). But of these 934, 648 had a spell on the dole, 759 lost status and 780 lost money in their new jobs.

These were the sort of reasons why workers and unions feared redundancy. What was it like being made redundant? Firstly these cotton workers were unusual in that they did receive some compensation for losing their jobs – most workers received nothing more than a week's notice. Where they did receive compensation, the amount was usually very small, a pound or two for each year of service was about the going rate. It was said that one of the things that angered the cotton workers was the way they were made redundant; cases were pointed to where people's cards were simply left on their machines without a word of explanation. The others still remember the dreaded 'tap on the shoulder' when the foreman told them their name was on the list. Another frequent complaint was that workers first heard about redundancy by reading it in the local paper. Certainly it was rare for employers to see redundancy as a subject for negotiation, or even consultation, with workers and their union representatives.

Union resistance to redundancy

The trade union movement as a whole did not see redundancy, or rather fighting redundancy, as one of its main priorities during the 1950s. As one writer put it, 'Pre-occupied as they were with gaining improvements in wages and conditions, most union officials were apparently content to collude with employers in keeping the whole thing in low key.' (Santosh Mukherjee *Through no fault of their own. Systems for handling redundancies in Britain, France and Germany* (Macdonald, 1973)). But this is not the whole story. It has already been suggested that behind a lot of the restrictive practices adopted by workers lay a fear of future redundancies and a desire to preserve jobs. Throughout the period there were also some dramatic fights against mass redundancies. One of the centres was the motor industry.

Redundancies in the motor industry In the post war years the motor industry developed a reputation for strong trade union organization, high wages and an aggressive attitude to trade union action. But behind much of this militancy were the powerful memories of much harder times. In the interwar years the growing car industry was known for being the home of seasonal labour. When demand for new cars fell during the summer months, many car workers, especially the semi-skilled ones, were laid off and then, if lucky, given jobs in the autumn when the demand for cars picked up again. This not only meant that their earnings were very unstable, it also made it very difficult to build up continuing trade union organization. This very insecure position was radically altered by the war when the car factories were turned over to the production of arms for the government. Many car workers were then working twelve hours a day, seven days a week. Additionally, as we saw earlier, the government took a much more favourable attitude towards trade union membership. Car workers came out of the war much stronger although this varied considerably between different firms and parts of the country. After the initial disruption caused by the switch back to peacetime production, the motor industry expanded rapidly with almost unlimited demands for cars in Britain and a strong position in overseas, and Commonwealth markets.

By the mid-fifties, however, the storm clouds were gathering. The motor industry was always the first to suffer when the government used financial measures such as tightening hire purchase restrictions and increasing purchase tax to 'put the brakes on the economy'. On top of this the technology of car production was changing rapidly especially with the introduction of the transfer line. In 1956, these two factors combined to lead to mass redundancies, firstly at the Standard Motor Company in Coventry and soon afterwards at many of the BMC factories throughout Oxford and the West Midlands. In each case thousands of workers were 'given their cards'.

In both cases the shop-stewards led strikes to try to save the jobs, saying that any drop in demand should be met by work-sharing rather than sackings. The willingness with which workers in other parts of the country offered financial support to the teams of strike committee members who toured the industrial areas suggested that the strikes had struck a chord. However, neither of these strikes were successful in their bid to save jobs. They both ended with the employers agreeing to pay compensation to some of the workers who lost their jobs; a solution that had never been put forward by the strikers.

But this was an episode in an important tradition of resistance to redundancy. There were a number of other long and bitter strikes for example:

● workers at Wickmans in Coventry – five weeks in 1958;
● workers at British Light Steel Pressings in Acton – eleven weeks in 1961.

Although rarely particularly successful in themselves, they had a profound effect on attitudes and policies towards redundancies amongst unions, employers and the State.

In the late fifties, unions began to become much more aware of the problem of redundancy although attitudes towards it remained divided. In the engineers' union (AEU) to which many of the strikers belonged, the policy-making national committee passed a resolution in 1957 instructing their executive council to 'conduct a national campaign against redundancies and for the right to work'.

Additionally they warned employers that 'this union will move into action to safeguard the livelihood of our members and will demand the right to work, and that the necessary action will be taken to enforce our demands'.

Within the unions, however, attitudes towards how the threat of redundancy should be met varied strongly. That resolution expressed the carworkers' view that unions should always try to preserve jobs and offer work-sharing as an alternative to sackings. Others, however, picked up the concept of compensation and argued that workers should be much more effectively cushioned against the loss of their jobs.

Employers too were strongly affected by shop-floor hostility towards redundancies. Although they usually won the actual strike the price in terms of lost production, bad publicity and damaged relations with their workers was often high. Other employers preferred not to lay people off rather than face that kind of a conflict.

In the late fifties, then, employers began to move away from seeing redundancies as something that they imposed unilaterally on workers and showed a greater willingness to try to reach some kind of agreement with their representatives. This involved giving longer notice, consulting about 'who' and 'when' and being prepared to pay slightly more generous severance payments to those who were made redundant. In some cases redundancy agreements were made with unions, these outlined detailed procedures to be followed in the event of redundancies as well as specifying the level of compensation payments.

Perhaps the most significant development though was the growing interest of the State in this subject. At the end of the decade at the time of labour shortage in some areas and industries it was felt that the government had some obligation to improve labour mobility. The Ministry of Labour began to collect information about how employers dealt with redundancy as part of a preparation for working out their own role.

119

In the 60s, the State takes a hand

It is perhaps worth beginning by looking at the various ways in which the State can affect the area of jobs.

Firstly as an employer it can have a direct effect either by employing more workers or by sacking, or attempting to sack, people. We have seen earlier how the State as an employer has expanded significantly since the war. At the same time, many of the industries with highest redundancies were controlled by the State. We saw earlier how the mining and railways had their work-forces virtually halved during the sixties; both were, of course, nationalized industries. As we shall see later, the way the 'State as employer' approaches redundancies can not only affect employment amongst State employees but also affect the thinking and policies of private sector employers.

Secondly, the State as a legislator can significantly affect the way employers and unions deal with redundancy. Below we will examine the effect of the Redundancy Payments Act and those sections of the Employment Protection Act dealing with redundancy consultations; but other laws are relevant, for during this period the 1964 Industrial Training Act and the introduction of earnings related unemployment benefit were both relevant to the policies being pursued.

Finally the activities of the State in its growing role as planner can have a very direct spin-off in terms of jobs. There are two outstanding examples in the sixties: the government's policy of encouraging mergers led to a process of rationalization in a number of sectors in which large numbers of jobs were lost. Secondly, as was seen in the previous chapter on living standards, in trying to plan wages the government actively encouraged productivity deals. These deals frequently involved significant changes in the internal labour market (the relationship of jobs within the workplace) as well as a, usually, indirect effect on that outside by reducing recruitment into many workplaces.

First steps   At the end of the fifties, beginning of the sixties

120

there were two industries in which the State took a more active role in relation to redundancies.

The first was in the cotton industry. It was seen earlier how there was a steady loss of jobs throughout the fifties in the industry. This pace was suddenly quickened at the end of the decade. The impetus here came from the government through the 1959 Cotton Industry Act. Its intention was to make the industry more efficient and better able to compete with foreign competition. The Act provided for government financial assistance for firms that scrapped old machinery as well as subsidies to help buy new and more modern equipment. As part of this scheme, the government insisted that workers who were sacked as a result of the scrapping of the old machinery should be paid some compensation out of a fund subscribed to by all cotton industry employers. In the seven months of the scheme thirty-eight thousand compensation payments were made. The impact on the people who received this compensation was noted earlier.

The railways were another industry that contracted quickly at this time. In the fifties, British Rail had operated a 'no redundancy' policy. They had run down the size of the work-force by other means such as 'natural wastage' (the non-replacement of staff who left) and through the willingness of railways workers to accept quite a high degree of labour mobility rather than lose their jobs. In the sixties, the intention was to reduce the work-force's size more rapidly, starting in the railway workshops. In 1962, British Rail and the unions came to the Workshop Redundancy Agreement in which BR abandoned their no redundancy policy and offered a detailed scheme in which workshop workers who were sacked received compensation. Under this scheme, the work-force was reduced by 30 per cent in two and a half years.

The Redundancy Payments Act (RPA)

The 'lesson' that the car industry employers drew from the strikes in the fifties was that compensation could draw the sting from shop-floor resistance to redundancies. The cotton and railways – and soon the coal industry – illustrated how very substantial redundancies could be carried through with very little opposition if they were linked to a severance pay scheme, or 'copper handshake'. It was these successful experiences that informed the Redundancy Payments Act that was introduced in 1965.

This Act still in a slightly modified form – provides the legislative framework for redundancy today, along with certain additions introduced in the Employment Protection Act. It needs to be understood against the background of the State's desire to assist in the breaking down of shop-floor resistance to redundancy and mobility of labour. The Act provides a national compulsory scheme of compensation for certain categories of workers if they are made redundant. It is financed through a redundancy fund to which all employers contribute. Employers making workers redundant claim half the cost back from the fund. The most important categories of workers who do not receive compensation under the Act are people over retiring age, part-time workers and those with less than two years continuous employment. Compensation paid is related to age, length of service and earnings at the time of dismissal. The maximum payment under the Act is thirty weeks pay for a person over sixty-one with at least twenty years service. In practice average payments under the Act have been very modest, for instance in 1977 the 267,234 workers who were eligible received on average only £619. It has always been open to employers to offer additional payments although they would have to fund them themselves.

In moving support for the Bill in Parliament, the Minister of Labour at the time set out its objectives quite clearly, it was:

. . . an active policy to make it easier for workers to change their jobs in accordance with the needs of technological progress . . . to ensure the planned use of resources, especially our reserves of manpower . . . an important complement to our efforts to develop the science-based industries and to deploy our manpower resources where they can make the most effective contribution to the economy.

Ray Gunter, cited in R. H. Fryer *Redundancy, Values and Public Policy*, Industrial Relations Journal, Vol. 4, No. 2.

It was designed to fit in with the government's other objectives by helping management use labour more efficiently within the workplace and encourage workers to leave declining industries and move to expanding ones.

Increase in the number of redundancies

There is no really accurate information on the rate of redundancies in Britain. In fact, before 1965, no official figures were kept at all. Any picture has to be built up from periodic surveys, labour exchange records and press reports.

- A NEDC survey, for example, suggested that the rate of redundancies in the 1956–8 period was about 200,000 a year.
- A Ministry of Labour study in 1962 suggested that in that year there were between 470,000 and 590,000 redundancies

After the RPA came into force, detailed records were kept but these were records of payments made under the Act. Still no systematic records were kept of people who were made redundant but received no payment under the Act such as workers with less than two years service and part-time workers. Yet very often these people were most likely to be made redundant. For example, a government survey relating to 1968 suggested that for every redundant worker qualifying for a payment under the RPA – between two and three redundant workers left empty-handed. Using this ratio, the number of redundancies that year would be between 750,000 and one million. Since then the number of paid redundancies has tended to rise and we could realistically be talking about an annual rate of one million redundancies. That is one in every twenty to twenty-five jobs going every year. This sharp rise in the rate of redundancies was, however, accompanied by a startling drop in the number of strikes against redundancy. In 1969, the government commissioned another survey, this time on the effects of the RPA and this revealed a noticeable drop in the number of anti-redundancy strikes although the overall strike rate was rising. In the five years prior to the Act, over 5 per cent of working days lost through strikes were accounted for by redundancy strikes. In the four years following the Act, the average figure fell sharply to below 2 per cent. Figure 13 shows what happened in particular industries.

Many of the redundancies which took place in the late sixties met with little or no resistance from the unions concerned. This could often be explained by the existence of

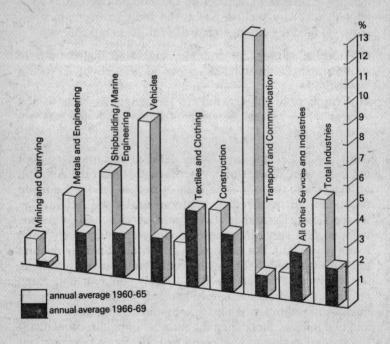

Figure 13 Redundancy strikes per annum as a per cent of all strikes.

Source: S. R. Parker, C. G. Thomas, N.D. Ellis, W. E. J. McCarthy 'Effects of the Redundancy Payments Act' HMSO, London 1971.

severance payments. The experience of workers in GEC provides a good example of this.

GEC

In 1967, the Government encouraged, and financially assisted, the merger of GEC with AEI and English Electric forming the largest private manufacturing company in the country with a work-force at that time of 181,000. On 1 February, 1968, it was announced that the old AEI telecommunications factory at Woolwich was to be closed with the loss of over five thousand jobs. The shop-stewards and union members at the factory reacted immediately. They began a campaign to keep their jobs. This included marches, lobbies, demonstrations and the potent threat to prevent any of the Woolwich machinery being moved.

The campaign did not succeed, however. In order to gain the acquiescence of the workers in the shut down, GEC offered relatively large compensation payments. By a narrow majority this was accepted and the factory was closed. This closure was just the beginning of a process of closures and rationalization which was to cost on average thirty redundancies per working day. An incomplete list of GEC redundancies in the following two years is shown on p. 126. None of the other workers on this list received as good terms as the Woolwich workers.

Why was resistance to redundancy weakened?

We've seen how the introduction of the Redundancy Payments Act was followed both by an increase in the rate of redundancies as well as a decrease in union resistance to them. What was happening? In 1966, one engineering convenor expressed his fears about the effects the existence of compensation payments was having on the attitude of union members towards accepting redundancy:

One of the real dangers at ENV and one that will pose a problem elsewhere, is the Redundancy Payments Act, which dangles a carrot

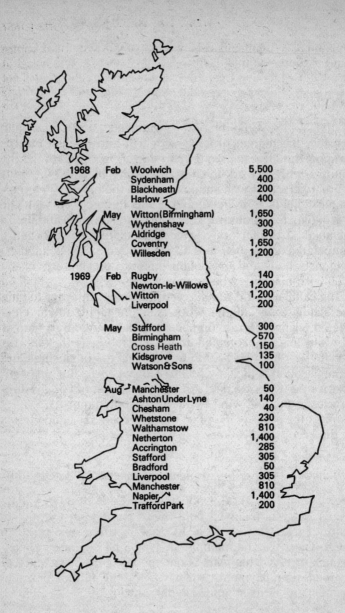

1968	Feb	Woolwich	5,500
		Sydenham	400
		Blackheath	200
		Harlow	400
	May	Witton (Birmingham)	1,650
		Wythenshaw	300
		Aldridge	80
		Coventry	1,650
		Willesden	1,200
1969	Feb	Rugby	140
		Newton-le-Willows	1,200
		Witton	1,200
		Liverpool	200
	May	Stafford	300
		Birmingham	570
		Cross Heath	150
		Kidsgrove	135
		Watson & Sons	100
	Aug	Manchester	50
		Ashton Under Lyne	140
		Chesham	40
		Whetstone	230
		Walthamstow	810
		Netherton	1,400
		Accrington	285
		Stafford	305
		Bradford	50
		Liverpool	305
		Manchester	810
		Napier	1,400
		Trafford Park	200

Source: CIS Anti-Report on GEC

in front of long service workers. For men with twenty years service a sum of £500 to £600 is very tempting. But when it is looked at logically, this payment, which comes only once in a lifetime will not compensate workers in a well organized factory, especially if they have to change their jobs and find that the alternative means a cut of £8.10s. a week in their wages.

The carrot of the lump sum led some workers to want redundancy rather than fear it. Many substantial reductions in labour were achieved through what has come to be known as voluntary redundancy. But is this an accurate term? A revealing remark was made by a twenty-two-year-old engineer who lost his job in the Clydeside shipyards in 1970.

I learned what it's like not to have a job. You understand better about unemployment when you've had the experience yourself.

He then continued,

I volunteered to become redundant myself mainly because of the atmosphere. Nothing was actually said to me but the feeling of the men, that you were last in and so should be the one to go, got through.

Quoted in Frank Herron, *Labour Market in Crisis: Redundancy at Upper Clyde Shipbuilders* (Macmillan, 1975).

Whilst this was perhaps an unusual case, it is worth recalling the sort of process that precedes 'voluntary' redundancy:

- rumours and statements are circulated about the poor prospects of the firm;
- rumours (again) circulate about the massive sums available for those who go, invariably maximum sums are quoted;
- often a spell of short-term working begins in which union members begin to accumulate debts which a 'lump sum' could wipe out;
- the employer invites people 'who are interested' to say so, then the number who do so are used to show how impossible it is to resist.

The work-force is then softened up for the actual negotiations with the results invariably being less lucrative than people had been expecting.

It is not only the members but also their representatives who are softened up. Previous collective resistance to redundancy was underpinned by an awareness of the damage done both to the sacked workers and to those who remained. Their organization was weakened and their productivity often increased. Management often tried to break up a united response by publishing the names of those to be made redundant. Nonetheless, steward resistance would be stiffened by the desire to defend the members whose jobs were threatened. In this new position the pressure is reversed. The possibility exists of dealing with a redundancy threat without anyone being forced to go. Given that redundancy has always been very difficult to fight, this is obviously an attractive option.

Employers have responded to this by showing a much greater willingness to negotiate about redundancy rather than simply declare it. This has been strengthened by legal requirements on employers under the Employment Protection Act to give unions notice of intended redundancies, to consult with them and to provide them with relevant information. Whilst stewards have remained aware that redundancy still means less jobs for the community as a whole as well as harder work for those who remain, their ability and willingness to take a positive no redundancies stand has been blunted by these changes.

In this sense, though, the RPA was a flexible weapon as employers who did not feel under pressure from unions could still make workers redundant at very little cost. As we saw earlier, the most vulnerable groups, workers with little service and part-time workers, had no statutory compensation.

It would be wrong to try to look at jobs in isolation from the other issues and problems faced by trade unionists and their representatives during this period. We saw in the previous chapter on living standards how a succession of incomes policies encouraged unions and management to negotiate productivity deals. These deals often affected the number and content of jobs in a workplace. For instance, one aspect of the famous productivity deal at the Esso Refinery at Fawley was the abolition of craftsmen's mates; another was greater flexibility between skilled grades. In the seventies, wage policies often put limits on the increases payable to particular groups of workers; individual workers could benefit by reducing the number of workers in the group either by redundancies or natural wastage. Many of the 'self-financing productivity deals' were simply this: sharing the work, and the pay out between fewer people. Stewards faced conflicting pressures in this situation. At a time of rising inflation they were under pressure to maintain living standards. On the other hand they wished to guard against job loss and deteriorating working conditions.

An important feature of trade union struggles during the sixties was the increased resistance to lay-offs, which were common in some industries like cars. Employers responded to a downturn in demand by putting workers on a two-, three-or four-day week, or sometimes sending them home in the middle of a shift. People were also laid-off because of shortages of materials and components. This made their earnings very unpredictable and led to demands for guaranteed earnings or lay-off pay. Often these were included as part of the productivity deal packages. However, experience with them has been mixed. Many trade unionists complain that management simply provoke strikes rather than pay for workers to be laid-off.

It is worth asking whether the RPA really helped meet the government's objectives. It certainly helped employers get rid of workers; in fact in its early years the fund invariably went into the red and had to be bailed out from central government funds. But many of those made redundant found it difficult to get jobs where their skills were used or work in industries which were, supposedly, expanding. In the seventies the inadequacies of the RPA became clearer. In this decade the problem overall was not lack of labour mobility but lack of jobs.

What's been happening to jobs?

In the first chapter we traced the relationship between changes in occupational structure (the sort of jobs that people do) and trade union membership. It was noted that certain industries, such as agriculture, railways, mining and textiles, had lost hundreds of thousands of jobs whilst others, particularly in the service sector, had expanded. In addition there had been important changes within industries: the rapid growth of white collar jobs being the most significant. Up until the end of the sixties, the supply of jobs had more or less kept pace with demand. Unemployment was not a major problem. Thus, between 1948 and 1966, the average number of people on the unemployed register was 350,000, or rather less than 2 per cent of all employees.

Starting in the end of the sixties, the pattern changes starkly. Although there were fluctuations, unemployment grew steadily. Between 1967 and 1974 registered unemploy-

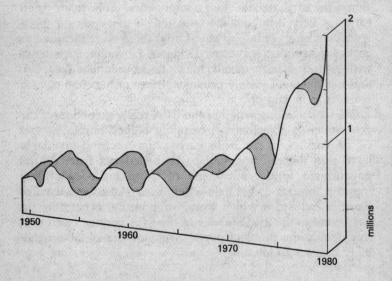

Figure 14 Unemployment since the war

Source: Unemployment: the fight for TUC alternatives, TUC, 1981

ment never fell below half a million. In 1975 it passed one million and has never fallen below. At the time of writing, the seemingly 'impossible' figure of two and a half million has been exceeded. This grim picture is illustrated in Figure 14.

A wider and wider gap opened up between the number of jobs available and the number of people seeking work. There are a number of inter-related explanations for this:

- changes in the structure of industry;
- increases in the number of people seeking work;
- the direct and indirect consequences of Government policy;
- technological change.

Restructuring Firstly, the number and types of jobs available continued to changes as illustrated by Table 11.

Table 11

Employees in Employment, 1970 and 1979			
	June 1970	June 1979	Change
Agriculture	454	354	− 100
Manufacturing	8164	7025	− 1140
Other production	2083	1945	− 140
Services	11,293	12,997	+1700
TOTAL	21,993	22,320	+320

(totals in thousands) taken from MSC Annual Report 1979.

Although there has been a modest increase in the number of jobs, it is much less than the demand for them. To understand the nature of the growing unemployment that has resulted, it is necessary to look at the changes in employment patterns in slightly more detail. Firstly there is the loss of over a million jobs in manufacturing industry. This happened right across manufacturing industry not just in the supposedly 'old' industries such as shipbuilding and heavy engineering and those known to have intense problems such as the textile industry. Table 12 gives some examples of job loss that had taken place by the mid-seventies.

131

Table 12

Industry	percentage jobs lost 1965–76
Food, drink and tobacco	10
Petroleum products	15
Chemicals	5
Metals	27
Mechanical Engineering	14
Electrical engineering	10

This contrasts with the first twenty years after the war when employment in many sectors of manufacturing did go up, albeit slowly. Increasingly trade unionists have been concerned that this trend represented not a natural 'adjustment' to more modern techniques in industry and more emphasis on services generally but a process of *de-industrialization*. It is feared that the country's productive capacity, and with it several million jobs, are being destroyed.

It is also helpful to look more closely at the category of service industry. This represents a wide variety of different jobs such as:

● banking, finance and insurance;
● many government employees such as workers in education, the Health Service and the Civil Service;
● employees in the private sector in areas like hotels and catering, entertainment, etc.

A growing labour force Secondly, the size of the 'working population' grew by over a million.

Table 13

Working population*	June 1971	June 1979	Change
Total	24,546	25,740	+1190
Men	15,838	15,681	– 160
Women	8708	10,059	+1350

(totals in thousands) taken from MSC op. cit. p.9
*The working population consists of the employed labour force plus the registered unemployed.

Table 13 highlights one of the main reasons: more and more

women were coming out to work. Many of these are married women anxious both to maintain the family standard of living and to enjoy the greater freedom and independence that outside paid employment brings. A million more women have gone out to work in the course of the seventies. Again we saw in the first chapter how many of these women joined the trade union movement and helped to extend union organization and activity in areas like local government and white collar factory jobs. The other main contributor was the increase in the number of school leavers following the increase in the birth rate in the early 60s. In 1975–6 637,000 school leavers were ready for work compared with a half a million six years earlier.

Government Cuts Government policies, especially since 1976, have had an increasing effect on employment in the second part of this sector. Since then the policy of expanding public sector employment has given way to a succession of attempts to cut public expenditure. As the unions with many members in government employment pointed out in 1976, this has severe implications for jobs:

It is abundantly clear from the examples that we have quoted that local government is cutting its labour force in all parts of the country and that the standard of service to the community is being reduced. Throughout the country vacancies are not being filled and staff over sixty-five are being laid off: and major job losses have taken place amongst particularly vulnerable groups of part-time workers, such as home helps, school crossing patrols and school mid-day supervisory assistants. Other groups who have been particularly at risk include road maintenance staff and ancillary workers in residential establishments and schools, architect office staff, surveyors and engineers.
('Breakdown: The Crisis in Your Public Services', National Steering Committee Against the Cuts.)

In a pamphlet published three years later by two civil service unions, it is estimated that cuts had already led to the loss of 200,000 jobs. ('Cuts: the other side of the picture' (CPSA/SPCS))

New Technology   There is another time bomb ticking away under jobs in both the public and private service sector. This is the possible impact of 'new technology'. The potential of computer technology using microprocessors to replace jobs is enormous as was seen on page 26 when we looked at some predictions. An area particularly threatened is what is known as the 'information' sector. By 1978, more than eight million people were involved in collecting, assimilating, storing, processing and distributing information. Many of these jobs can be taken over relatively cheaply by computers. A recent union report listed some of the jobs likely to either disappear or be transformed in the next ten years:

Post room workers	Sales clerks	Draughtspeople
Typists	Stock clerks	Computer operators
Secretaries	Progress chasers	Programmers
Invoice clerks	Data preparation staff	Accountants
Filing clerks	Cashiers	Supervisors
Shipping clerks	Telegraph operators	Administrators
Stores clerks	Warehouse workers	Junior and middle managers
Insurance clerks		

Many of these jobs are in those areas, like insurance/finance, local government employment, etc. which have until recently been the main growth areas, especially for women workers.

Union activity and unemployment

This severe rise in unemployment presents unions with their toughest challenge. Unions have always seen full employment, the *right to work* for all workers, as one of their central aims. The traumatic and shattering experience of the thirties served to underline this emphasis. And yet this goal, which appeared to have been achieved in the first twenty years after the war, seems to have slipped away. We saw how unemployment passed half a million, one million, a million and a half and now two and a half million. It is rapidly becoming again a permanent, built-in part of the system we live in.

Who then are the unemployed? Statistics in themselves do not tell the whole story of unemployment. There are the personal tragedies of the unemployed themselves. Stories of going without, of children suffering because there is no money in the house. Stories of a non-existent social life and hence losing touch with friends and former workmates. Daily more and more people are finding that there is no solution to the pressing and increasing financial problem of being unemployed.

For some groups of workers being thrown out of work is and always has been a familiar experience. Some workers are considered more expendable than others. For example, registered unemployment amongst women has risen much faster in recent years. Since 1975, male unemployment has increased by 61 per cent but female unemployment has risen by a staggering 207 per cent. The problem is even greater when you consider that as many as 50 per cent of women seeking work do not register and are not officially numbered amongst the jobless. Many women work in insecure, low paid, part-time jobs which are often the first to disappear. Young and old alike also suffer disproportionately when jobs are scarce. In 1966, 25 per cent of the unemployed were under twenty-five, by 1980 this figure had risen to 50 per cent. The position of unskilled workers is increasingly precarious. Throughout the 1970s the unskilled have borne the brunt of rising unemployment. In times of job shortage, vacancies for 'general labourers' are few. Workers from among the ethnic minorities are often the first to be laid off and the last to be taken on. Furthermore, unemployment is not evenly distributed throughout the country. In Liverpool, for instance, 40 per cent of those on the register have been unemployed for more than a year, compared to 26 per cent nationally.

The gravity of the situation is underlined by the fact that more people are spending a longer time out of work. In 1975, 14 per cent of the unemployed had been without a job for over a year, by 1979 this figure had reached 25 per cent.

How have unions responded to this challenge in the seventies? We can look at this in two ways: firstly, the efforts of

135

workplace union organization to stop unemployment at source by resisting redundancies and closures, secondly, there has been the increasing attempts by unions nationally to reverse government policy and encourage state action to save jobs.

Unions at work 1970–74 We have already seen how previous government action, notably the Redundancy Payments Act helped weaken union resistance to redundancies. Resistance was not, however, extinguished. Trade unionists continued to try to find ways to maintain their jobs. The following pamphlet, written by a group of Bristol trade unionists, suggested a number of ways in which this could be done:

STAGE 1 – IMMEDIATE REACTIONS TO THREATS OF REDUNDANCY

A Policy of Resistance

Faced with a redundancy threat the trade unions must first establish and consolidate a POSITION OF POWER DERIVED FROM THE TRADITIONAL WEAPONS OF COLLECTIVE BARGAINING.

(1) Organisation

- (a) set up a joint trade union committee representing all trade unions in the establishment.
- (b) prepare a joint policy based on a rejection of unemployment by redundancy.
- (c) set up a fund for administration costs, leaflets etc.
- (d) establish contacts and continue liaison with trade union officials, district committees, trade councils etc., essential contacts and information to and from other associated establishments, local firms etc.
- (e) establish contacts and exert pressures through other organisations, Government Departments, M.P.'s, local authorities, the press etc.
- (f) prepare detailed reports on overtime in other establishments within the group and local industry etc., a survey of all sub-contract work, employment of outside agency workers, prospects of employment within the firm and the locality.

(g) continual involvement of membership – by mass meetings – publication of broadsheets/news flashes etc., to sustain policy.

(2) Immediate Sanctions

(a) All overtime working to cease.
(b) No recruitment of new staff.
(c) Review and control over all sub-contract work and the employment of outside agency workers.
(d) A stop on all transfers and mobility within the establishment.
(e) Working without enthusiasm.

(3) Further Sanctions which may be necessary

(a) Work sharing.
(b) Shorter working week.
(c) Work-to-rule.
(d) Specific, controlled and well-timed one-day or part-day token demonstrations.
(e) 'Blacking' of any activities by those not supporting the agreed policy.

In the final analysis the situation might demand that the legitimate interests of the workers can only be met by a withdrawal of labour and there are many many redundancy situations where this has proved to be the case.

These trade unionists felt that after the Conservative Industrial Relations Act, unemployment was the most serious threat that the movement faced. Certainly by the early 1970s this view seemed to be becoming more widespread.

During this time unemployment rose very quickly and the newly elected Heath Government set its face against government support for firms facing financial problems. It was known as the 'lame duck' policy. The graph in Figure 15 illustrates how strikes against redundancy became more frequent.

Strikes were only one response: other actions like overtime bans were not recorded. Also left out of the statistics were some of the more direct and imaginative approaches used by workers of which the forerunner was the 'work-in' by the UCS shipyard workers in 1971.

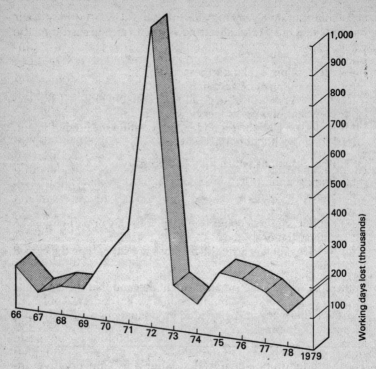

Figure 15 No. of working days lost through strikes on Redundancy Questions, 1966–1979.

Source: D of E Gazette

UCS

The shipbuilding workers on the Clyde illustrate how particular groups of workers were suffering severely from the rise in unemployment. For years their industry had been losing jobs and local unemployment was high; for example 10 per cent of Clydeside's workers were out of work. For these people the link between redundancy today and unemployment tomorrow was a clear one. Already, many of their former colleagues who'd been sacked from the yards the year before had either settled for inferior jobs or were still looking. No doubt an awareness of this underlay their reaction when a government appointed commission into the yards, reporting in the summer of 1971, concluded 'any continuation of Upper Clyde Shipbuilders in its present form would be wholly unjustified and would cause serious and widespread damage'. They recommended that UCS should go into liquidation. Of the eight and a half thousand workers then employed, six thousand would have to go.

Sensitive to the fact that their bargaining position was weak, the shop-stewards committee proposed a different course of action to a strike. They suggested to a mass meeting that they should work-in: everyone should turn up for work and carry on making the ships in the yards. The uncompleted ships were a strong bargaining counter and this action would provide a positive base from which to campaign for the retention of their jobs. This was accepted and for nine months the work-in continued. Men who had been declared redundant by the government's liquidator were paid instead out of a fund administered by the shop-stewards. This fund paid out nearly £9000 a week.

The ability of the shop-stewards to raise money on that scale signalled the support they were getting from trade unionists elsewhere. Workers all over the country rallied round. And the support was not simply financial – mass demonstrations and sympathy strikes were held in the West of Scotland.

The work-in ended in the spring of 1972 when an American firm, Marathon, took over the yards. A substantial number of jobs were saved although at the price of tough productivity deals.

This more aggressive, and optimistic, approach to threatened redundancies was noted elsewhere. At the Plessey factory in nearby Alexandria, on Merseyside at the Fisher Bendix works and motorcycle builders in Coventry; these and other groups occupied their workplaces or 'worked-in' rather than see the work go away. These actions certainly helped to stem the tide. A number of workers' cooperatives were formed, and lasted for some years. In fact the Triumph cooperative near Coventry is still in existence. Resistance to redundancies was part of a rolling tide of opposition to government policies which included the massive pay strikes of the miners and the TUC's campaign against the Industrial Relations Act, and at a wider level it had an effect. These pressures helped to push the government into changing course, modifying its 'lame duck' policies and pursuing more expansionary economic ones. For a time unemployment fell.

Unions and State policy, 1974–79

The change of government in 1974 accentuated a shift that was taking place already in trade union thinking on employment. The experiences of the 1970–74 period had brought trade unionists up against the problems of fighting unemployment within a market economy. The problems concerned both the nature of trade unionism (by their very nature unions tend to reflect the interests and pressures of employed workers) and the difficulties of bargaining from a position of weakness, when management wanted to get rid of workers because demand for the product was falling. This was particularly true of the period from the mid-1970s onwards. Look again at the graph on redundancy strikes and see how it tailed off as the seventies progressed. Invariably trade unionists ended up looking at the role of the government, demanding financial assistance for the firm or industry or, in some cases nationalization, to preserve their jobs. The unions nationally, with the TUC taking on a prominent role, increasingly emphasized the need to expand and alter the role of the State in the economy in the direction of policies that would protect employment. Prior to the Labour election victory, the unions had been closely involved with the drawing up of their economic policy which called for a much more active role for the State in resisting de-industrialization. The TUC too had been, since 1968, producing its own Economic Review offering detailed guidelines for union representatives on State bodies.

These policies took the expansion of employment opportunities as a central aim in a number of ways.

Reviving the manufacturing base For some years unions had been voicing their concern at the loss of jobs and productive capacity in manufacturing industry. They wanted to see the State take a much more active part in encouraging employers to invest more, export more and provide more jobs. The National Enterprise Board was seen as a key way of doing this as were planning agreements and a network of tripartite planning committees with the NEDC, nationally complemented by planning at an industry and company level. A lot of the pressure for industrial democracy came from the view that union pressure would push firms into adopting more expansionary policies.

Expansion of the 'social wage' As public sector cuts became a regular feature of government policy, especially after the 1971 loan from the International Monetary Fund, the defence of the social wage became an increasing union priority. Again this was linked to a defence of jobs in the public sector as well as an awareness of the link between cuts in public expenditure and job loss in private industry. Decisions to build less schools and hospitals meant less work for the construction industry and the manufacturing firms supplying materials and equipment.

Manpower planning These aims were relatively long term and the unions did not expect unemployment to disappear overnight. They constantly pressed the government both to ward off redundancies, through measures like 'temporary employment subsidies' and to assist the unemployed through increased 'job creation' and training measures. Although the government has been willing to adopt some of these measures, unions have generally been frustrated in their attempts to radically alter their thinking even when Labour was in power. The NEB, which was intended to take an interventionist role in a substantial minority of private manufacturing industry, has been largely concerned with the problem of restructuring British Leyland. Planning agreements have hardly been used and unions have complained at the modest role taken by the sector working parties.

141

More recently the 'alternative economic strategy' has been fed back more deliberately into collective bargaining. For example, the steel unions, faced with the run-down of their industry, have begun to campaign for an alternative strategy for the British Steel Corporation, including a 10 per cent cut in prices in order to counter declining sales. In terms of resisting unemployment, perhaps the most significant development has been the building up of union pressure to reduce working hours with the intention of reducing the supply of labour and forcing employers thereby to take on more workers. In 1979, the engineering employers agreed to a staggered reduction to a thirty-nine-hour week. Now about five million manual workers are covered by agreements giving them a working week less than forty hours and most of these have come since the engineers' settlement. Unfortunately these small cuts in hours do not seem to have had much effect in terms of creating jobs. In 1980, however, unemployment continued to rise and we will return at the end of the book to looking at the impact this may have on trade unionism in the eighties.

Key points

- Unions have found it increasingly difficult to defend their members right to work and protect job security.
- The so-called restrictive practices adopted by unions have provided an important means of defending jobs.
- Unions in the fifties did not see massive redundancies in industries like cotton as a major issue and were content to settle for compensation for those workers who were thrown out of work.
- One group of workers, in the motor industry, took an alternative view and struck in order to try to save jobs.
- In the sixties the State as both an employer and legislator had a considerable impact upon the redundancy issue.
- The State adopted a policy of trying to breakdown workplace resistance to redundancy in order to encourage the mobility of labour.

- The Redundancy Payments Act, passed in 1965, was the mechanism through which some workers were guaranteed a legal entitlement to compensation for the loss of their job.
- The introduction of legal compensation in the sixties was followed both by an increase in the rate of redundancies as well as a decrease in union resistance to them.
- The lack of resistance to redundancy invariably weakened union organization and left the individual worker with only a temporary financial gain and no job.
- In the seventies the problem overall was not lack of mobility but lack of jobs.
- The rising unemployment of the seventies was due in the main to industrial restructuring which entailed massive job loss; an increase in the labour force, the deliberate policies of successive governments and technological change.
- Some groups of workers, in certain areas, have suffered more than others from rising unemployment, among them are women, ethnic minorities and school leavers.
- Resistance to redundancy in the seventies took many different forms – the example of UCS encouraged a spate of redundancy strikes, occupations and work-ins in the early part of the decade. Workers' co-operatives were seen as an alternative to redundancy.
- In the last six years unions have tried with limited success to influence government policy in the direction of creating more jobs and aiding the unemployed. They have advocated different economic solutions to those favoured by the last Labour and current Conservative administrations.

Discussion

- How many people are employed at your workplace now compared with five years ago?
- Why do you think unions have been unsuccessful in resisting the rise in unemployment?
- What alternatives are there to redundancy?

Further reading

At the time of writing the TUC has just published a pamphlet called, 'Unemployment: the Fight for TUC Alternatives', which we recommend you read. It costs 50p from the TUC.

Many public sector unions have brought out pamphlets arguing against cuts in public spending. A good example is, 'The Other Half of the Picture', by two civil service unions, the CPSA and the SPCS.

Reading about the struggles of unemployed workers in the thirties is still useful. They are well described in Wal Hannington's classic, *Unemployed Struggles 1919–36*, which has recently been reprinted by Lawrence and Wishart.

Chapter **six**

Health and safety at work: a new priority?

So far we have looked at how unions have responded to members' demands for a better standard of living and greater job security. You would probably agree that these are two of the most important reasons why people join unions. This chapter is about how people have, through trade union activity, tried to protect themselves against hazards at work.

It will show how health and safety has emerged as an important trade union concern. There are a number of reasons why this should be so:

● Because of their jobs working-class people die younger

and experience worse health than the rest of the population. Periods of sickness involve not only physical suffering but also financial hardship.

● Accidents happen the whole time at work. There are the regular toll of cuts and bruises that many workers have come to see as 'normal'. Still too frequent are the major tragedies: the construction worker falling a hundred feet, the drowning fishermen or the crushed and suffocating miners.

● New threats to health and safety emerge almost daily. Many of these hazards are developed in laboratories, power stations and chemical works. Look at the way visual display units have swept through offices in the last few years. Nobody examined beforehand their possible effects on people's eyesight.

These things have been said many times before but little has been done to get rid of the problems.

Trade unionists have always been reluctant to accept that this is an inevitable situation. They've felt that work could be made both healthier and safer. Employers have not always agreed, especially if the cost of making improvements was high. But for trade unionists the fight for a better working environment ought to be a priority. There's no point in having good pension schemes if most of our members die soon after they retire. High piece-work earnings are all right, but if they mean taking risks is the cost too high? How often have you had to cancel a night out because you felt exhausted, had a headache, backache or eyestrain? All of these problems could have originated in work.

The ways through which trade unionists have tried to tackle dangerous working conditions have changed considerably in the last thirty years. It is only in the last few years that we have had workplace safety representatives appointed by unions. And the initiative came from the State, through an Act of Parliament. This is an interesting contrast to the way in which other aspects of workplace trade unionism developed. As we saw in Chapter two, this was largely stimulated by events at work; the law played no role at all.

In this area too, the impact of the changing composition of the work-force and of trade union membership, made itself felt. Workers, for example in the service sector, found that the structure of legal protection left them out. Office workers, health service workers, people working with new technology began to demand through their unions the same sort of protection as miners and foundry workers.

This chapter focusses on the development of health and safety as an important trade union issue. In particular it will:

- Look at the different ways that trade unionists have traditionally tried to fight for healthier and safer workplaces.
- Suggest some reasons why attitudes towards health and safety changed, especially in the sixties and seventies.
- Look at the introduction of the Health and Safety at Work Act and safety representatives with legal powers.
- Ask some questions about the effect these changes have had on the actual conditions in the places where union members work.

Union traditions and health and safety

Organizing against dangerous and unhealthy working conditions has always been part of the role of the trade union movement. This has been especially true in heavy physical jobs like underground mining, steel smelting or shipbuilding. But despite the obvious dangers, workers like the miners have always faced an uphill struggle trying to get their employers to make the job as safe as possible. When their union was weak, safety standards suffered. For example, in 1937 there was an appalling mining disaster in Gresford in North Wales where 265 miners were killed. Less than a third of the miners at the pit were union members. After investigating what happened, the Chief Inspector of the Mines, remarked on the necessity of strong trade unionism to prevent the recurrence of this kind of tragedy. He said,

I hope I am not exceeding my function in saying now what I have held for many years, that miners should be members of some effective trade union. That opinion is based on grounds of safety, with which I am alone concerned, for I believe a well organized trade union, wisely directed, can be as potent an influence for promoting greater safety in mines, as it is already in matters, for example, of wages and conditions of employment.

(Quoted by Michael Foot in moving the Health and Safety at Work Bill.)

Aware that they would not survive long by trusting the mine owners to protect their lives and limbs, miners had for many years elected their own workers' inspectors. These miners regularly checked safety standards in the pits and inspected sites of accidents. As the miners suffered the consequences of their defeat in the 1926 General Strike and the impact of mass unemployment, these workers' inspectors found it almost impossible to be effective. They received little help and frequent harassment from the mine owners and their representatives. The mines were nationalized after the war and seven years later, in 1954, a new Mines and Quarries Act was introduced which gave the workers' inspectors the legal right to undertake their functions.

Workers in other dangerous jobs were often not so effective. Did you know that one of the jobs with the highest proportion of fatal accidents is agricultural work? Or that people working in kitchens suffer from twice the average rate of deaths from pneumonia? Neither of these occupations have strong trade unionism in the workplace. Dangerous work is a feature of most jobs. Let's now look at the way in which most workers have responded to this threat.

Compensation

The hallmark of the traditional approach is the fight for compensation. Many people, when they think of industrial accident or diseases, tend to automatically ask the question: can I get any compensation? Indeed one of the most powerful reasons often given for union membership is the assistance provided in the event of an accident. The State, through the national insurance scheme, does provide a system of industrial injury benefit and long term disability benefit. These are similar to, although slightly higher than, State sickness benefits. However, where a worker can prove, through the courts, that the accident/disease was caused by his or her employers' negligence or breach of the law, then the employer has to pay compensation to the injured person.

To win compensation can be an expensive and long-winded process. Employers are insured against claims and the insurance companies usually resist them, however strong the member's case. Alternatively they may play on his or her immediate financial problems and offer a modest 'out of court' settlement. Unions all provide members with free legal assistance, often from lawyers experienced in handling industrial accident claims. As well as this, an important part of the activities of shop-stewards and branch secretaries has often been helping members pursuing claims. This involves informing members of their rights, getting hold of the relevant forms, seeing the accident details have been properly recorded, finding witnesses and providing relevant information, like a sketch or photograph of the accident site, for the solicitor.

This represented an important part of union activity but it was very much a case of too little too late.

Legal protection

In the more positive area of prevention, there was a tendency by unions and shop-floor workers to rely on the law for protection. A good example of this approach can be seen in the history of the foundry workers.

Campaigning for safer foundries   One section of manufacturing industry where the workers have always been aware of the hazards they face is foundries. The foundry is where the rough metal castings are made for use in the engineering industry. The process involves melting metal in huge furnaces, pouring it into moulds and then, as the metal cools, 'knocking it out' in its shaped form. It doesn't take much imagination to see the sort of damage that molten metal can cause people if they come into contact with it. But this is just

149

one of the threats facing foundry workers. The atmosphere is often full of the sand that is used to make the moulds. This gets into the lungs causing crippling diseases like silicosis. The air too is full of fumes, carbon monoxide from the hot metal and toxic fumes from the materials used to make the cores that go inside the moulds. On top of this, the work is very noisy as many of the processes, like the knockout, involve the constant clatter of metal banging against metal. Foundry workers often start going deaf at a young age.

In the years following the Second World War, the damage that these conditions were doing showed up in the statistics. In 1950, the accident rate (at 3.95 per 100,000 man hours worked) was nearly twice the industrial average. In 1957, government figures showed that foundry workers suffered 30 per cent more sickness than other occupational groups. For some illnesses the differences were even more dramatic. The incidence of rheumatism and arthritis was 100 per cent higher, of bronchitis 80 per cent higher and of stomach disorders 40 per cent higher. Death rates in the age groups, fifty-five to sixty-four were 30 per cent above the national average.

Through their union, they continued to fight back. Changes they were looking for included:

● stricter control over 'housekeeping': items like clear gangways, smoother floors and safe stacking and storage of materials;
● better washing and welfare facilities;
● vastly improved ventilation to reduce people's exposure to toxic fumes and dust;
● efforts to make the foundry a quieter place in which to work.

In common with many workers they looked to the law to lay down standards for their employers to obey. In doing this they were continuing a union tradition stretching back to the early nineteenth century. The 1937 Factory Acts (which were revised again in 1961), were a cumulation of legal reforms that owed much to trade union pressure. They laid down strict requirements on employers to control certain hazards:

for example, the guarding of machinery and the regular testing of lifts and lifting equipment. In other areas they were less strict, however, and some hazards, like noise, were not covered at all.

The foundry workers wanted the Factory Acts extended to give detailed requirements for the specific hazards we looked at above. A report in 1947 had suggested a number of ways in which foundries could be made safer. The union wanted these made into regulations under the Factory Acts. Six years later new regulations were introduced and they went some, although by no means all, of the way towards meeting their demands. Stewards and branches were issued with a health and safety handbook reprinting the regulations alongside the union's own safety policies. Workplace representatives were being used to act as safety watchdogs, trying to see that their employer stuck to the law.

Workplace action

What the foundry workers were finding was that getting better laws was only the beginning. Employers often ignored them or else found loopholes. Many requirements were qualified by the statements 'where practicable' or 'where reasonably practicable' and this often provided ample room for employers to find excuses. This was why the foundry union encouraged branches to appoint safety delegates to help keep the pressure up. This was unusual in that in most industries this was left to shop-stewards and little help or guidance was given. Where unions did take safety issues up with their management, the response was often lukewarm and sometimes hostile. Faced with this, the foundry workers and others came to the conclusion that if workplace safety representation was to work it needed legal backing. The rest of industry needed to copy the miners.

In 1964, supported by other unions whose members worked in hazardous industries, such as the construction engineers (now the construction section of the AUEW), they managed to convince other unions at the TUC that this was the way forward. The resolution reprinted here was passed despite the opposition of the TUC General Council.

1964 Congress Resolution on Safety

Congress declares that in order to provide effective safety organization in industry, the Factories Act should be extended to provide for:

(a) The election of safety delegates, with powers of inspection, by the workers concerned in factories; such powers of inspection to include the right to inspect the scene of an accident and the equipment involved, a right at present available only to miners under the Mines and Quarries Act 1954;
(b) the setting up of safety committees in factories;
(c) the right of workers' safety delegates to accompany the factory inspector on his visit to factories;
(d) the advice of the factory inspector to the firm to be available to the safety committee or safety delegates.

Source: 1964 TUC *Annual Report*.

Although largely hidden from the public eye, the seeds of this tradition of workplace action in other industries were already being sown. Shop-stewards and staff representatives took up hundreds of thousands of individual issues: when it was too cold in winter or too hot in summer, oil or water on the floor, having to handle metal with dangerous burrs or sharp edges, dangerous lifting tackle, heavy manual lifting, badly designed or non-existent machine-guards. All these, and many other problems cropped up the whole time and they were seen as part and parcel of the shop-stewards' job. Sometimes they led to disputes. Many a group of paint-shop workers walked out when the fumes became intolerable. Often jobs were blacked until the equipment was safe. Frequently groups insisted that two people should do a job because it was dangerous done alone. In many workplaces, too, a few of the stewards became health and safety enthusiasts, went away and studied the Factory Acts and tried to mount sustained campaigns to improve working conditions.

Failings of the traditional approaches

We've already seen how the laws were patchy, strong on some items but weak on others, and they were, in any case, frequently ignored by the employers. The only external means of enforcement was the factory inspectorate. But the small band of inspectors were quite incapable of policing the factory laws. They were so stretched that they could only visit the 'average' workplace once every four years. When they did find breaches of the law they rarely prosecuted and even then successful prosecutions led to derisory fines as these two extracts from the Robens Report show.

Extracts from the Robens Report. (July 1972).

More generally, it is also evident that despite the existence of voluminous legal requirements, only a very small proportion of offences ever lead to prosecution. On the evidence of these figures, the Factory Inspectorate is the most active of the inspectorates in bringing prosecutions; and according to factory inspectors it is rare for any inspection visit not to reveal a number of breaches of the law for which criminal proceedings could be instituted. Nevertheless, some 300,000 visits made by factory inspectors in 1970 result in the prosecution of less than 3000 offences [paragraph 259].

Broadly speaking, present maximum fines range from £300 for certain offences, under the Factories Act to £50 under the Acts dealing with safety in agriculture. In practice, magistrates rarely, impose the maximum fine. In 1970, for example, the average fine imposed for safety and health offences under the Factories Act was £40. Even the smallest firm is unlikely to find this onerous. [paragraph 258].

Thus the existing system claimed to offer workers two types of protection. There was in some industries, factories, docks, mines, construction and some others, a partial framework of legal obligation on employers. And workers were entitled after they'd had an accident to claim compensation

153

from their employer, although they often didn't get it. But individually and taken together, it was a quite inadequate system. A look at the graph in Figure 16, which shows accident rates in the 1960s, suggests that it created little effective pressure for improvements in working conditions.

Workplace trade unionists involved in health and safety were also confronted by an additional problem. This was in convincing their membership that health and safety really mattered. Within the workplace there were constant pressures to trade safety off against other priorities. Many a safety issue ended up with an agreement to pay 'danger money' and often incentive payment systems encouraged groups of workers to 'choose' between money and safety. All these pressures kept the subject at the fringe of trade union activities.

In order to remedy these inadequacies, two strands of policy were developing in sections of the trade union movement: the demands for stronger and more detailed obligations on the employers and the legal right for unions to

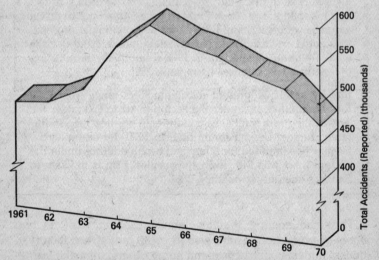

Figure 16 All accidents at work in Great Britain 1961–70

Source: Robens Report. p. 162

appoint safety representatives. Commitment to these issues did of course vary considerably but there was a growing recognition amongst trade unionists that their approach was not sufficient.

New hazards . . . new workers

Particularly in the 1960s, the growing frustration amongst workers in the traditional 'dangerous occupations' was added to by two significant forces. These were new groups of workers and the hazards they faced. These workers greatly stimulated pressure within the unions for more attention to be paid to health and safety questions.

We saw in Chapter one how the composition of the work-force was changing significantly, with a rapid expansion of jobs in the service sector and in white collar employment. Most of these 'new workers' were not covered by any protective legislation at all. It was not until 1963, with the passage of the Offices, Shops and Railway Premises Act that there was any comprehensive legislation covering the growing numbers of office workers. And most of the people working in the service sector, public and private, were not protected at all even though many of them were exposed to serious hazards.

An injured foundry worker would be rushed to the casualty ward of the nearest hospital. Ironically many of the people working to ensure his recovery would themselves be exposed to serious risks in the course of their daily work. Just think of the ambulance workers and porters, rushing patients into hospital, in close contact with people who may be suffering from a (as yet undiagnosed) serious infectious disease. The risk of infection spreads to the nurses; the cleaners and laundry workers handling bed-linen; and to the people in the laboratories working on the analysis of specimens. Infection is just one source of risk. Health service workers suffer from many similar problems to others: dangerous machinery in the kitchen, laboratory and laundry, toxic chemicals (from cleaning liquids to anaesthetics), cuts from 'sharps' like scalpels and hypodermic syringes. Nursing

155

is one of the occupations suffering most from backache, often caused by lifting patients. No wonder one of the main unions in the health service, NUPE (National Union of Public Employees), was demanding – in a 1965 resolution accepted by the TUC – that their members be brought within the scope of legislation.

When the Health and Safety Executive conducted a survey into conditions in hospitals, they highlighted what many hospital workers were already finding out; hospitals were riddled with asbestos;

Asbestos lagging has been widely used for insulation of steam, hot water plant and pipework. Numerous examples of abrasion were found, e.g. in boiler rooms, underground service ducts, kitchens (on calorifiers).

Asbestos is a good example of an aspect of health and safety that became more prominent in people's minds. Many of the hazards of work did not lead to sudden injury: the loss of a hand in a machine, asphyxiation from fumes or severe burns from an electrical accident. Often damage was not noticed at the time. Workers were being slowly killed but it would be ten, twenty, thirty years before they knew. The medical community had known for years that asbestos dust was a killer but its use increased dramatically after the war. Millions of trade unionists came into contact with it, at work and at home. Gradually an awareness grew.

One incident that brought this home to many people was the exposure of the conditions at a factory in Yorkshire which made asbestos products. The factory had opened in 1939 and closed in 1970. Of the 2200 people who had worked there, it was discovered that 12 per cent had developed crippling asbestos disease. The factory was covered by the Asbestos Regulations but these totally failed to protect the workers there. The publicity given to this and other incidents alerted trade union members to the possible dangers facing them. Many groups of workers took action:

● dockers refused to handle asbestos imports;
● building workers demanded proper equipment to work with asbestos products;

- workers in hospitals, factories, schools and universities insisted that asbestos lagging be removed or effectively sealed;
- groups who worked with asbestos, such as laggers (insulation engineers) campaigned for better conditions.

These experiences were leading many people to ask questions about their working conditions. They wanted more information about substances with which they worked, they wanted more control over their working environment and tougher laws to provide protection. Gradually this pressure was forced up through the union movement.

- Members of the TGWU working in the rubber industry discovered that people were dying of liver cancer because of a chemical they worked with. The TGWU went along to the TUC demanding tougher laws governing the use of toxic chemicals.
- Workers in the furniture industry were spurred into action by a tragic fire. They too came along pointing to the gross inadequacy of the fire protection laws.

Different groups of trade unionists, then, were expressing their discontent about health and safety and their determination to see some change.

The Health and Safety at Work Act

We've seen how there were two strands to the union policy which reflected this pressure. Firstly the law should be strengthened to provide a stricter framework of legal obligations on employers, backed up by more factory inspectors and bigger fines. Secondly, after the 1964 debate, the TUC was committed to campaigning for legalized safety representatives and compulsory safety committees. The first Wilson Government began the process of reform in 1967 by circulating a consultative document that broadly reflected TUC policy. Later, in 1970, a new Bill was introduced but it was lost when Labour was defeated in that year's election. At the same time a committee, chaired by Lord Robens, was set up to provide a comprehensive survey of health and safety and make recommendations for legal reforms.

In moving slowly towards change, Labour was partly bending to union pressure. But there were strong reasons why the State found the present situation unsatisfactory. The administrative and legal set up was a mess: there were a number of different inspectorates responsible for enforcing different laws. There was a mines inspectorate, a factory inspectorate, an explosives inspectorate, an alkali inspectorate, whilst some areas were inspected by local authorities or the fire authorities. This led both to particular confusions as well as a general difficulty in developing any unified State policies to improve conditions.

For as we saw earlier, in one very important way, the system was failing; accidents continued to rise. The costs of this both to employers and the State was very high. Calculations undertaken for the Robens Committee estimated the cost of industrial accidents and diseases to be between eighty and a hundred million pounds a year. The cost to the State included hospital costs and benefits to injured workers and their families. The main cost to employers was lost production. Another estimate for 1970 compared days lost through strikes, accidents and sickness:

● ten million days lost through strikes;
● twenty million days lost through accidents;
● three hundred million days lost through certified sickness.

Robens reported to the Heath Government in 1972, but little immediate interest was shown. Again, a Bill was introduced right at the end of that Government's period of office. It was this Bill, however, which was to form the basis of Labour's Health and Safety at Work Act, which was one of the first major pieces of legislation introduced by the 1974-9 Government. Robens, the Labour and Conservative Governments agreed that there should be a shift in emphasis to the workplace if health and safety was to be improved. The role of the State should be to stimulate reform at workplace level.

But there were important differences between employers and unions. The overall employers' view was that specific duties and obligations should be replaced by a general duty of care with more emphasis on the duties of employees. Union policies still argued the need for specific obligations on employers. On the question of safety representatives, the employers were willing to see greater 'worker involvement' but reluctant to see this either as legally enforceable or as the sole prerogative of the unions.

The Act finally fell somewhere in between. All workers were brought within its scope by a system of general duties on all employers towards their employees. The way the Act is designed to work, and can be used by trade union members, is described in another book in this series, *Health and Safety at Work*. The employers welcomed this system whereas many trade unionists and some Labour MPs felt the duties were too general; they particularly objected to the constant use of the term 'so far as is reasonably practicable' which they argued would enable employers to wriggle off the hook. When it came to safety representatives the Act leant towards the union view. It allowed for regulations to be made which would give trade unions the right to appoint safety representatives and call for safety committees. This acceptance of trade unions as the single channel for worker involvement was an important example of the procedural gains made by trade unions at this time. The Conservatives had wanted to leave open the option of non-union appointment of safety representatives. Trade unionists too were pleased at the commitment to increase the size of the Factory Inspectorate, now re-named the Health and Safety Inspectorate, and give them the right to issue Improvement and Prohibition Notices.

Safety representative regulations

We saw that the Act gave government the power to introduce regulations legalizing safety representatives. The process of drafting them was left to the Health and Safety Commission a newly created body with trade union, employer and State representation. A draft was circulated for consulation in late

1975 and it was expected that the regulations would come into force in May 1976.

The proposed regulations, with an accompanying code of practice and guidance notes, presented an interesting model. They drew both on the experience of miners and on that of the labour movement in other countries, particularly Sweden, but they also recognized the extremely varied and decentralized nature of British trade unionism. The proposed regulations enabled all recognized unions in a workplace to appoint safety representatives. These representatives would have certain legal rights, which included:

● to inspect the workplace every three months;
● to inspect accident sites;
● to receive certain types of information;
● to inspect certain documents;
● to consult with the inspectorate;
● to investigate complaints from, and represent, members;
● to call for the setting up of joint safety committees.

The regulations laid down this general framework of rights and functions but the initiative was left with workplace trade unionists to claim their rights and negotiate their detailed application.

Many trade unionists, who as we saw earlier, were keen to become much more involved in workplace health and safety, looked forward to the regulations giving them the right to do so. They were rather alarmed therefore when the summer passed and there was no sign of the regulations coming into force. A question from an MP, prompted by a local group of health and safety activists, unearthed the fact that the Government intended to postpone indefinitely their implementation. The reason was that the Local Authority employers were fighting a last ditch stand. They claimed that the implementation of the regulations would cost them £80 million; a figure that surprised the Health and Safety Commission whose own estimate was less than £3 million.

The announcement of the postponement triggered off a furious reaction. Union leaders felt that the Government had broken a central part of their social contract commitments.

Local activists felt they'd been led up the garden path. The force of the reaction was sufficient to push the Government into giving a definite date for implementation: October 1978

What has happened since October 1978?

From October 1978, union members in every workplace where they were already recognized by their employer, were entitled to appoint safety representatives. This was a new departure. Existing workplace organization, the growth of which we looked at in Chapter two, developed outside of any legal framework. The stimulus was provided, by and large, from events inside the workplace. The introduction of a different payment system requiring local negotiations, technological change that altered the way a job was done or a management initiative that caused resentment; events like these encouraged groups of trade unionists to elect someone to speak on their behalf. Over time this grew into a developed organization, learning ways of working, coordinating activities, keeping in touch with members and talking to management. Not surprisingly, the map of British workplace trade unionism is a very varied one. No two organizations are quite the same, each has built up their own traditions and ways of doing things.

In contrast to this, the initiative for safety representatives came from outside the workplace, in fact from an Act of Parliament. The regulations both provided the main stimulus and a framework through which trade unionists saw the main functions of their safety representatives. Whilst the new powers were welcomed, many people were worried that this departure could cause serious problems for trade union organization. Unions had, after all, invariably opposed any interference by the law in industrial relations at work.

What did they fear? An extract from the Robens Report gives us a clue,

Indeed there is a greater natural identity of interest between 'the two sides' in relation to safety and health problems than in most other matters. There is no legitimate scope for 'bargaining' on health and safety issues, but much scope for constructive discussion, joint

161

inspection, and participation in working out solutions. (paragraph 66)

Would health and safety be used to resurrect the notion of consultation that had fallen into disuse in most industries? Trade unionists had usually lost interest in consultation because it rarely delivered the goods. Would health and safety allow it in through the back door? Would health and safety too emerge as a complex and technical issue, with union 'experts' working closely with employer and State 'experts', using a language not understood by ordinary trade union members?

The first thing that we we can say about the unions' response is that, where they were already well organized, trade unionists seized the opportunity to use their rights and appoint safety representatives. Within the first year of the regulations coming into force, an estimated 100,000 safety representatives had been appointed. There can be little doubt that the speed with which this took place revealed considerable pent-up demand for more trade union action on health and safety. Nationally the trade union movement, and especially the TUC's own education department, encouraged this with a massive programme of education for newly appointed representatives.

The regulations, in a way, by-passed national union organization by placing the initiative at the workplace, although union leaders had been closely consulted in the framing of the regulations. Union head offices were, however, active in advising their local representatives about how best to use their new rights. Usually they warned of the dangers of allowing health and safety to drift away from other aspects of union organization. The following extract from the TGWU's handbook is a good example.

It is union policy that, wherever feasible, all safety representatives should be union shop-stewards. The advantages of this are obvious: stewards are already the elected representatives of our members with some responsibility for working conditions and accountability within existing Union rules and workplace procedures, custom and practice; furthermore they are already well organized, with long established relations with other stewards from our own and other unions at the

place of work and past experience of negotiations, grievance handling etc. On the other hand, the Union recognizes that there will be
the occasional instance of the appointment of someone other than
a steward being to the satisfaction of the Union members covered
and trade union organization at the workplace. (Paragraph 3/3)

This approach was generally adopted by workplace representatives although often in a modified form. Shop-stewards'
committees frequently tried to balance their desire to maintain control over health and safety with a willingness to bring
in some new enthusiasts, even though they might not be
shop-stewards. As we saw earlier, many shop-stewards were
already grappling with health and safety problems and welcomed the added 'muscle' which they felt the law would
now give them. In any case the introduction of the Health
and Safety at Work Act took place at a time when steward
influence in other areas was declining. Incomes policy severely restricted work-group influence over pay, and health
and safety provided a welcome opportunity to make progress
in a different area. The overall impact was really to stimulate
workplace representatives into a more thorough and vigor-
ous approach to 'health and safety bargaining'. The build up
of trade union pressure on noise is a good example of this.

Noise: health and safety bargaining in practice

People have been going deaf because of noisy conditions
since the industrial revolution. It is estimated today that over
a million industrial workers are exposed to dangerous noise
levels. Despite this, it was not until 1971 that a worker suc-
cessfully sued his employer for damages because of negligence in exposing him to noise. Frank Berry, a worker in the
shipbuilding industry, was awarded £1250. The next year,
the Government issued a Code of Practice advising employers on the steps they should take to reduce the exposure to
noise of their employees. For some time unions with members in noisy jobs, like the Boilermakers, had been campaigning for more legal protection.

The significance of the arrival of the safety representatives
was that this type of problem was increasingly taken up on

the shop-floor, directly with management. For example, in Coventry, large numbers of workers in the motor and engineering industry worked in noise levels that were slowly damaging their hearing. Often, it was only when their safety representative came back from a TUC course that people realized why they had difficulty hearing the television, or thought that their families didn't speak clearly enough.

This prompted frequent discussions amongst shop-floor workers about the need for rapid improvements. In one car factory, workers on a particularly noisy cylinder boring machine, agreed that their shop-steward should ask management to find ways to reduce the noise. Getting nowhere they threatened to turn the machines off after they had had a maximum safe 'dose' of noise every day. This would have meant stopping them after two or three hours. Under pressure, management agreed to spend some money: defective parts were replaced, noise-absorbing booths and silencers were fitted and the machines were mounted on damping material.

In a nearby components factory a press operator developed a nasty ringing in his ears that kept him awake at night. After a visit to the specialists, he approached his union, wanting to sue the company for compensation. The ringing in the ears was a disease called tinnitis, caused by exposure to high noise levels. Elsewhere in the press shop, encouraged by some of their stewards, operators began to refuse working on some of the noisier presses until something was done. The shop-stewards committee brought in the factory inspector and slowly remedial action was taken.

Health, safety and control

These are just two examples of a process that was taking place all over the country. Safety representatives and stewards began asking quite new questions about their work. What's in this bleach that gives us sore throats whenever we use it? What's that strange smell whenever the machine overheats? What are the effects of spending eight hours working as an audio-typist? Flowing from these sort of questions came demands for much more information about processes and substances used at work as well as for greater involvement in areas of work that had previously been left to management.

Concern about noise has led to stewards questioning the design of the machine as well as its location. From that it led to the need to have some control over the choice of new machinery so that similar problems didn't keep cropping up. Worries about the ingredients in glues and solvents suggested questions about precise composition which had hitherto been assumed to be 'trade secrets'. Again, the problems needed to be stopped at source. Safety representatives, wanted to know when a new substance was being introduced into work and to be convinced that it was safe before it was used. These were quite new areas for most workplace representatives to be probing.

Safety representatives pursuing apparently straightforward problems encountered two types of resistance. 'Cost' was invariably put up up as a reason why a hazard couldn't be removed. Secondly, the challenge to managerial control was resented and resisted. It became clear that the obstacles to a healthier and safer workplace were much more deep rooted that many trade unionists had at first imagined.

Management responses

We saw how the Health and Safety at Work Act was designed to influence the behaviour of both trade unionists and management. The Act required all employers to draw up safety policies that outlined both their approach to health and safety and the means through which it was to be carried out. The view was that health and safety needed a much more central part in management organization. Safety committees were intended to link a re-vamped management structure to greater union involvement. Although managerial responses have varied, the overall response seems to have been more cautious and conservative than that of trade unionists. Certainly, reports from the Health and Safety Executive have

165

expressed disappointment over the failure of the safety policy to radically alter management behaviour.

What management has had to do is respond to the growth of trade union pressures. It has just been suggested that the response has often been slow and reluctant. In this they have been assisted by the broad nature of the new duties imposed upon them; a difficulty which was anticipated by many trade unionists. But in coming to terms with greater 'safety militancy', a more distinctive managerial approach is beginning to emerge.

In their own evidence to the Robens committee, the Confederation of British Industry, argued that greater stress should be placed on the legal responsibilities of employees, not simply employers. In workplaces they have usually been quick to publicize those sections of the new Act which place general duties on employees. Arguments with safety representatives about hazards have often centred on where responsibilities lie. When union spokespersons have demanded better ventilation or safer machines, management have pointed to the need for workers to behave safely or wear protective equipment. On some issues, they've moved further, trying to enlist the support of union safety representatives to try to 'police' their members, seeing that they wear their glasses, helmets, boots, masks or whatever. These pressures have often proved important constraining influences on safety representatives.

The unions nationally

The Act, and the regulations, put the emphasis on trade unionists at the workplace. But local attempts to build safety organization along with greater participation by unions in national policy-making machinery placed new demands on trade unions as national institutions. Their main experience had been in the field of providing legal assistance with accident claims. Their major response to the arrival of the safety representative was the mass provision of education and following this the publication of handbooks and 'model agreements'.

Trade unionists looked to a variety of sources for assistance in coming to terms with the new requirements placed on them by health and safety problems. In many industrial centres, like Sheffield, Liverpool and Coventry, they formed area health and safety committees to exchange experience and information. In search of technical assistance, sympathetic scientists in universities, and sometimes in industry, were approached. Members of the British Society for Social Responsibility in Science provided a valued source of help and a regular flow of relevant publications on workplace hazards.

A number of unions, however, have appointed additional full-time officials, to specialize in the area of occupational health and safety. The GMWU, for example, now has a national health and safety officer along with health and safety officers in every region. This has enabled them to give much more back up to GMWU safety representatives and brief national officers involved in policy formulation.

This development also recognized the fact that health and safety is not simply a question of local 'trouble-shooting'. There is a need for national initiatives to lay down standards which all employers will maintain. This was what many trade unionists hoped the law would do in the past. The Health and Safety at Work Act encouraged the development of a series of tripartite committees (unions, employers and State) that could agree on standards which would then take the form of regulations and codes of practice. With greater expertise, and local experience, unions have been able to take a more active role in these committees.

Their experience, however, has been mixed. Returning to noise, the structure of tripartism did not allow for any agreement on what should be the recommended noise level. Employers' representatives argued that the unions' proposals would be far too expensive. For their part, unions replied that the employers' standards would still cause considerable hearing damage to many union members. The unions, through the TUC, have now decided to campaign for their own policies. Publicizing their views widely amongst union members, they hope to achieve through bargaining with employers what could not be gained at the national level.

This was how one union, ASTMS, saw the situation facing trade unionists who wished to improve noise levels.

The HSC approved the setting up of a new tripartite working party on Noise, and this held its first meeting amidst high hopes for an early recommendation in November 1976 . . . Initially the TUC nominees on this working party . . . argued for a noise exposure limit of 80dB, in accordance with TUC policy. By the end of 1976 they were holding out for an interim target of 84dB to which the 'independent' members of the working party gave their assent. . . . This proposal is unacceptable to the employers' representatives on the working party, who are intransigent and will brook no weakening of the 1972 limit of 90dB. The working party is completely deadlocked.

This is almost a classic case study in the failure of tripartite mechanisms for negotiating health and safety regulations. The whole tripartite edifice comes toppling down once employers adopt intransigent positions. The stand-off can be resolved in one of two ways: either the government can intervene and issue legislation on its own authority – a most unlikely eventuality – or the Trade Unions themselves can declare the standards they wish their members to aim for, and then back these standards with their industrial muscle. ASTMS Policy Document: 'Prevention of Occupational Deafness, Control of Noise at Work'.

Workers who came into contact with the pesticide 245-T began to discover it had horrible effects. The Agricultural Workers' Union compiled a dossier revealing massive evidence of miscarriages and deformed babies amongst women who'd come near it. They wanted its use banned. The Pesticides Advisory Committee, however, were not satisfied that the evidence they presented was conclusive. The agricultural workers, along with other unions whose members were involved, were not satisfied. They persuaded the TUC to take direct action; calling on trade unionists to ban the use and import of the stuff.

Health and safety in the future?

The issue of health and safety illustrated the ability of the trade union movement to react speedily to new demands. Their response involved the development in six years of new organizations and the modification of existing ones. As trade unionists directed their energies and resources, at work and in the national arena, to this problem, it emerged as an issue of clear conflict between them and their employers.

This experience of health and safety poses two vital questions for the future. Firstly, can this commitment to health and safety be maintained in the face of many other immediate, and sometimes, contradictory pressures which workers now face? Secondly, can trade unionists show the same kind of enthusiasm and innovation in tackling the problems of unemployment and technological change that will dominate the eighties?

Key points

- The fight for healthier and safer working conditions has become an important part of trade union activity.
- Traditionally unions have approached this issue in one of three ways: pressing for compensation, legal protection and some improvements in working conditions. These proved inadequate means of dealing with the problem.
- The expansion of the work-force in new areas along with the discovery of new threats to health exposed still further the inadequacies of the system.
- Unions had two main aims: the legal right to appoint safety representatives and stricter legal obligations on employers.
- The State played a central role in initiating change. The 1974 Health and Safety at Work Act extended some legal protection to all workers and, in the 1977 Regulations, gave unions the right to appoint safety representatives.
- Trade unionists seized upon their new rights. 100,000

safety representatives were appointed and many new health and safety issues taken up.

● Generally, employers have been no more willing to concede in health and safety than they were on other issues. 'Health and safety bargaining' was the pattern that emerged.

Discussion

● Do you agree that health and safety is a major priority for trade unions?
● What has happened to health and safety in your workplace during the 1970s?
● How can unions best continue the fight for better conditions at work?

Further reading

In this chapter we refer to the fact that many unions nationally have produced material on health and safety. You may like to check and see whether your union has produced a general guide for safety representatives or information on particular hazards. In addition, the TUC has its own handbook on Health and Safety priced £1.

There are a lot of good pamphlets written by trade unionists. A review of workplace organization is contained in the WEA pamphlet. 'What's happened to Safety?' (60p from the WEA, 9 Upper Berkeley Street, London W1). The British Society for Responsibility in Science has produced a good series of pamphlets on major hazards. Their address is 9 Poland Street, London W1.

All of the above information is well presented and drawn together in another book in this series, *Health and Safety at Work* by Dave Eva and Ron Oswald (Pan, 1981).

Chapter **Seven**

Unions in the eighties?

In this book we have looked at changes which have taken place in trade union membership, organization and influence since 1945. In the space of these thirty-five years membership affiliated to the TUC has nearly doubled, a system of workplace representation has been consolidated and unions have bargained with governments about economic and social policy. Unions, through both action and achievement, can justly claim to have become the industrial voice of working people. This would be a very convenient summary if history did actually come to a full stop at the bottom of this page, which of course it doesn't. We are currently witnessing a major

171

revision of recent history upon which this book is based; it is therefore important that in this final chapter we explore these changes.

In the eighties, workers and their unions face their sternest challenge since the thirties. Growth and employment are now being sacrificed in order to combat inflation in a time of deepening recession. Behind this strategy lies a deliberate attempt to weaken trade unions. The post-war political consensus which brought unions in from the cold and has allowed them to flourish has been cast aside. Full employment which we briefly enjoyed during the 1950s and early 1960s has clearly been abandoned. Social and economic inequality has increased. The process of tripartite discussions has been curtailed as the Government has consciously ignored the views of the union movement. Opponents of unionism have welcomed this attempt to return us to the uncertain and hostile environment of the thirties. Will the development of unions described in this book prove short-lived? Or can we defend the advances we have made and move forward to improve them?

In this final chapter we look at the changes which are affecting trade unions in the eighties:

- the challenge to unions and union members;
- the changes which are already influencing union growth, organization and relations with the State;
- the likely impact of these changes upon the future of union power.

Challenge of the eighties

In 1979, the Conservatives came to power after a strong anti-union campaign. They were pledged to reduce union bargaining power and restore incentives to work:

The crippling industrial disruption which hit Britain last winter had several causes: years with no growth in production; rigid pay control; high marginal rates of taxation; and the extension of trade union power and privileges. Between 1974 and 1976, Labour enacted a 'militants' charter' of trade union legislation. It tilted the balance of power in bargaining throughout industry away from the responsible management and towards unions, and sometimes towards unofficial groups of workers acting in defiance of their official union leadership.

From the Conservative Party Election Manifesto, 1979

They certainly wasted little time in setting about the first of those election promises. The result is that, as we write, trade unionism is under the strongest attack from government for a generation. But how new is Thatcherism? We have already seen how, since the mid-sixties, governments have tried various ways of controlling union power. You will recognize many of them from our discussion in early chapters, they include legal attack on union rights, raising unemployment, cutting public expenditure and incomes policy. The present Government is distinguished by the fact that it is trying to implement all these measures at the same time with a ferocity that is reminiscent of governments in the 1920s.

Let's look in detail at each of these challenges.

Anti-union legislation

The Employment Act, passed in July 1980, marks the first step in what could be a series of anti-union legislation. Unlike Heath's unsuccessful attempt in 1971, the Employment Act does not try to alter the whole framework of industrial relations in one step. Instead it attacks key areas of union rights. The target is both rights of workers individually and their right to take action collectively through trade unions. The Act has three main purposes. Firstly, it reduces the right of all individual workers to claim unfair dismissal and women workers to claim maternity leave. Secondly, it restricts the rights of trade unionists to take industrial action by limiting their entitlement to picket and mount secondary or sympathetic industrial action in support of other workers. Thirdly, it is intended to weaken union organization by impeding attempts by unions to recruit new members and retain effective 100 per cent membership in existing workplaces.

If this particular piece of legislation fails in its intention to break down union organization, effectiveness and solidarity then there is a hint of worse to follow. Waiting in the wings since January 1981 has been a Green Paper on trade unions' legal immunities which discussed the wisdom of further restricting workers' rights to apply sanctions in disputes with their employer. Such divisive legislation would be on the statute book now if some members of the Conservative Party had their way. It will undoubtedly become a real threat if the present Government continues in power after the next election.

Unemployment

Since the late 1960s governments have tended to use unemployment as a tool of economic management and this has greatly intensified under the present administration. Since the beginning of our period there have been four bursts of unemployment in 1967, 1971, 1975–76 and the period since 1979. On each occasion the number thrown out of work has increased. The TUC estimate that this strategy, if pursued, could see the real level of unemployment, including those not registered, at around the five million mark by 1985. This might seem impossible, but would you have imagined in 1979 that unemployment could have risen by 1 million in two years? We saw in Chapter five the damaging effects which unemployment has had upon the individual worker and union organization. The Conservatives are far more concerned about the latter than the former. Unemployment is being used particularly in the private sector, as a new form of incomes policy. High levels of unemployment weaken workers' collective organization. Managements resist wage claims because of the threat of bankruptcy, workers fear losing their jobs, trade unions are unable to finance lengthy strikes and the workers that have jobs are forced to accept a cut in their living standards.

Cutting the public sector

It is not just workers in British Steel or BL Cars who are being forced to accept cuts in real wages, low paid hospital and local authority employees are facing similar problems. In the public sector the attack has come on three fronts. In the winter pay round of 1980/81 the Government set a target of a 6 per cent ceiling on pay awards for its own employees. This is considerably below the rate of inflation. Secondly, strict cash limits have been placed on public expenditure. This is leading to massive job loss and a reduction in the services provided. For example, in some areas the school meals service for children is being drastically cut, throwing hundreds of part-time women workers on to the dole queue. In addition, many areas of State industry and public services are being returned to private ownership. This has involved measures like the sale of profitable parts of British Rail and the extension of private practice in the Health Service. Both of which make the services in question less accessible to those who most need them. Thirdly, the whole basis of our system of social welfare is being undermined. The amount strikers' families can claim in supplementary benefit has been reduced. We all saw the hardship which this was intended to cause during the steel strike of 1980. The unemployed have also been adversely affected by new measures designed to cut their living standards to the bone. Earnings related benefit is being abolished in 1982. The real value of benefits will no longer keep pace with the cost of living. People being made redundant will find that their severance pay prevents them from claiming supplementary benefit.

Other challenges: multinationals and new technology

The more obvious threats posed by current Government policies should not mask the other changes which are taking place. The continuing concentration of capital in large multinational enterprises is one such example. Multinationals are now estimated to account for one third of world industrial production and one half of industrial trade. The present Government has lifted restrictions on the transfer of capital abroad which will accelerate this accumulation of wealth and power. It is not just foreign multinationals that pose problems for trade unionists. A recent survey by Labour Research showed that overseas production is a large and increasing part of the output of the fifty largest privately-owned manufacturing companies in the United Kingdom. Employment in these companies is increasing abroad but falling in this country. Multinationals, because of their sheer size, the resources at their command and their ability to move jobs around the world make the task of effective trade union organization particularly difficult. It is certainly not a case of British workers 'pricing themselves out of the market' as we are so frequently told. There is considerable evidence to suggest that multinational companies operating in this country see us as a comparatively cheap source of labour. British employees of multinationals enjoy less generous pay and conditions than that given to their European counterparts.

A second, and perhaps related, threat is the advent and adoption of new technology. Its application across a wide variety of jobs, from word-processors in the office to the robot on the production line, presents a challenge to workers' jobs, health and living standards. Thatcherism may well prove to be a temporary phenomenon; these other challenges will not.

Into the eighties: union growth, organization and the State

Just how will the challenges we have identified in the preceding pages affect the union movement, and how will it respond? To answer this question we turn again to the themes which were addressed in the first three chapters namely union growth, organization and political influence.

Union growth

As expected, rising unemployment has already begun to take its toll on union membership. Before the official opening of the 1980 Trades Union Congress, Len Murray warned that the next year would see a sharp drop in affiliated membership to well below twelve million. It is now clear that he was right. Early in December 1980, Moss Evans revealed that the country's biggest union, the TGWU, had lost 140,000 members in the previous year. In their Northern Region alone the union lost 7000 members and £180,000 in dues in the year ending in October 1980. Even ASTMS, which you will recall experienced rapid growth in its white collar membership, has suffered a small but uncomfortable drop of around 13,000 on a declared membership of 491,000 over the past year. Among the many small unions hard hit by the recession is the Amalgamated Textile Workers' Union which has seen a loss of about 5000 members over the past twelve months, leaving total membership at around 30,000 (*Financial Times*, 6 January 1981). All our unions have lost members irrespective of their size or occupations in which they recruit.

Since the mid-sixties, a steadily rising membership has provided the unions with a buoyancy and measure of financial security. In the eighties, a falling membership might well have the reverse effect.

New members? How are the unions meeting this challenge? In the first instance they are making a determined bid for more members. You will recall how in Chapter one we identified certain groups of workers who have in the past proved difficult to organize; the unions are now attempting to get these workers into membership. A recruiting leaflet from the GMWU illustrates the urgency with which new members are being sought (see pages 178 and 179). The task of recruiting new members in work will not be made any easier by the Employment Act referred to earlier. They can expect even stronger resistance from employers and greater interference from the courts.

Recruiting the unemployed Most unions, including the GMWU, allow unemployed members to pay a reduced subscription. Retaining the unemployed in membership is seen as a priority for the eighties. The bitter experience of the

CONSOLIDATE GMWU MEMBERSHIP AT YOUR OWN WORKPLACE

Where you have a Union Membership Agreement ("UMA" or "Closed Shop")

* ★ Check everyone supposed to be covered by the UMA is actually in the GMWU (or one of the unions).
* ★ Do this by:
  * ● Holding a **Card Check** for every section covered by a GMWU Shop Steward or Staff Representative on a given date **either**: a date to be given by Head Office:

    or: a date you choose yourself – make it a few weeks in advance so as to give due notice to those without a card.
  * ● Getting access from management to the payroll to check that all on the list are actually in the Union. **Approach those who are not.**
* ★ Make sure **all** new starters join the GMWU **immediately** on starting and it is a condition of employment.
* ★ Check if there are any groups not covered by the UMA who should be – for instance – ● Part-Timers ● Canteen Staff ● Cleaners

In All Situations

* ★ Get acccess to new starters as soon as they start – this can usually be arranged with management – preferably **before** they actually start.
* ★ Check that **all** groups on your site and within your employers control are in the Union.

  Check particularly:
  * ● Part-Timers
  * ● Canteen Staff
  * ● Cleaners
  * ● Warehouse & Ancillary Staff Workers
  * ● Workers in small outlying depots.
* ★ Where MATSA is not recognised, are the non-manual staff in a union? If not – notify the Region's MATSA Officer immediately.
* ★ Where there are sub-contractors on the site:–
  * ● Check whether they belong to a union:
  * ● If not, refuse to work with them until your employers have insisted on GMWU membership with all sub-contractors;
  * ● Inform your Regional Organiser of the name of the sub-contractor so he too can help.
* ★ Get the Shop Stewards at the delivery or in the loading bay to check all **drivers** for suppliers, clients and customers. If they are not in the union, insist they join the GMWU.

THE UNION MUST CONSOLIDATE TO STAY STRONG.

WHEN MEMBERS LEAVE THEIR JOBS – KEEP THEM IN THE UNION

Shop Stewards, MATSA Representatives and Branch Secretaries should try to make sure that when a member leaves his or her job, that does not mean a loss of a union member.

* If the member is changing jobs – get him or her to fill in a "Change of Job Card" (get one from Regional Office) and return it to the Branch.

* The Branch Secretary should then try to keep the member on the books by hand collection until it is clear what the union situation is at the new job In many cases the GMWU are or could be organised there.

* If a member is **moving house**, get the new address and do the same as above but notify the appropriate District or Region to which area he or she is arriving.

* If members are **retiring**, make sure they know about retired membership **(2p a week)** in the GMWU.

* If members are **unemployed** or **redundant**, remember even in these bleak times the Union may be able to give help and advice to unemployed members. The unemployed rate is 2p a week.

BRANCH SECRETARIES HAVE SPECIAL RESPONSIBILITY TO KEEP UP CONTACT WITH MEMBERS LEAVING THEIR JOB.

thirties, when the official union movement clashed with the National Unemployed Workers Movement, suggests that a new approach to involving the unemployed will have to be found. There are considerable difficulties in forging a new identity of interest between employed and unemployed people. Workers are constantly moving in and out of employment in a steady stream which prevents the growth of a permanent organization. Many of the long term unemployed are non-unionists, women, young and older workers who are going to be hard to recruit. Finally many employers will attempt to use the newly created army of unemployed people as the basis for a non-union labour force. Despite these drawbacks it is obviously important that we do involve the unemployed. The recent TUC Conference which resolved to establish Unemployed Workers' Centres to advise, assist and involve the unemployed marks a small step in that direction. The considerable success of the People's March for Jobs in May 1981 showed too the possibilities of building a mass campaign against unemployment.

Union mergers   The twin problems of a decline in membership and financial instability have convinced many unions that they cannot survive on their own. In the words of one union official . . . 'during periods of difficulty in the past union members have come to recognize that the old slogan, "Unity is strength", has particular force'. (David Norman, *POEU Journal*, 1981.) The trend of union mergers is not a particularly new one. Our period has seen a considerable amount of merger activity. The number of unions affiliated to the TUC has fallen from 191 in 1945 to 109 in 1980 during which time membership has increased by six million. There is evidence to suggest that we are about to see a further spate of mergers; take the Post Office as an example. Employment in the Post Office is threatened by the prospect of government action to reduce their monopoly on services, and by job loss through the introduction of new technology. A recent report commissioned by the Union of Communications Workers (the old UPW) predicted a loss of some 40,000 UCW jobs, a quarter of the union's membership in the 1980s. The unease which members feel about technological change has prompted both major unions in the Post Office, the UCW and the Post Office Engineering Union (POEU), to explore ways in which they can unite to provide an effective opposition to likely consequences of change and job loss. These unions are not alone in seeking organizational solutions, print and rail unions are seriously discussing mergers in their own industries. White collar unions like APEX and AUEW (TASS) faced with redundancies in engineering are also seeking new alliances. The boilermakers and agricultural workers are looking to improve their bargaining strength by joining forces with a bigger union.

Union organization

In the post-war years we have seen a considerable growth in both the size and scope of workplace bargaining. Trade union members, their shop-stewards and more recently their safety representatives have fought for and gained a measure of control over earnings, working conditions and safety. Direct job control of this kind forms the basis of trade union power. The strength of this organization will provide the only effective basis for defending our interests in the eighties.

Workplace organization, like the unions nationally, is having difficulties coming to terms with the recession. The power of trade unionists at work has obviously been weakened by the high levels of unemployment. Members have understandably been reluctant to take a tough stand on job conditions if bankruptcy seems possible and the chances of finding another job are slim. This fact more than any other has led to stewards and workers losing much of the control they exercised in the seventies.

The plight of workers in the West Midlands, home of the engineering industry, is a good case in point. Between October 1979 and October 1980 unemployment in this region has increased by 70 per cent and by the mid-eighties the area is destined to become one of the country's unemployment black spots.

In this climate, stewards in the car industry and engineering in places like Coventry have found it difficult to resist an erosion in their members' working conditions and living standards.

The balance of control over workplace issues has shifted back towards the employers. Most workers have accepted wage increases well below the rise in the cost of living. Greater managerial control is shown too in tighter discipline and greater mobility of labour. BL Cars is a well known example of management scrapping collective agreements that had operated for decades and imposing much less favourable terms. Perhaps most importantly, this weakening of trade union power has made resistance to redundancy very difficult and limited the ability of union members to secure adequate safeguards when new technology is introduced.

The absence of a coordinated reaction from ordinary workers and their representatives is in part reflected in a reduction in the level of industrial conflict. With a few notable exceptions there is little at present to suggest that workers are prepared to emulate the actions of workers at UCS nine years ago. Strikes, after reaching record levels in 1979, returned last year to a figure just below the average for the previous ten years. The bulk of the 11.9 million working days lost in 1980 were accounted for by the three-month national steel strike. This does not mean that there was no opposition. The official figures do not include political events like the TUC's Day of Action, strikes by aerospace workers over denationalization plans and the fisherman's strike over quayside fish prices.

The newly appointed safety representatives, considered in Chapter six, have also faced similar problems. Unemployment can also breed illegal working conditions. Many workers are tempted to accept jobs in which they forfeit all legal and trade union protection if the only alternative is no job at all. Employers have less cause to worry about safety standards. Cuts in expenditure imposed on the Health and Safety Executive mean fewer inspectors and less frequent visits. The introduction of microtechnology also presents dangers to those who keep their jobs. Safety representatives are not just confronted by the health hazards of new technology, but also have to cope with the dangers it poses for trade union organization in the form of increased managerial supervision and greater flexibility in the use of labour.

Breaking down old divisions – the union response

The picture is not all gloom. Important changes are taking place within the union movement that offer hope for future action. Historically, we trade unionists have found that one of the main obstacles to united action is that we are divided. Divisions which are created by the jobs we do, the way we bargain and the very way in which we are paid. Opposition is often fragmented and therefore ineffective. But remember the unions have changed a great deal since 1945. Now over 40 per cent of the TUC's total membership is amongst non-manual workers, women account for a third and public sector workers a half of those affiliated. Of course these three categories overlap but that does not alter the scale of the change which has taken place. The old divisions are beginning to break down in response to the challenges which we now face. Consider the following examples as being three of many. The introduction of new technology poses identical problems for staff and shop-floor workers, and provides grounds for joint action by their unions. Women workers react in the same way to redundancy as men. Increasingly women are to be found taking leading parts in industrial struggles. The experience of the last two years has once again shown workers in manufacturing that cutbacks in public sector expenditure mean a loss of orders for their workplace. They share with public employees a common interest in preserving and increasing investment in public industries and services. The union movement in the eighties is learning that 'solidarity' is much more than the name of a Polish union.

Unions and political power

The muted response that greeted the TUC's Day of Action in May 1980 caused many trade unionists to think long and hard about the ways in which opposition to government policies can be mobilized. The open hostility shown by the

Thatcher Government towards unions has virtually closed the door to joint discussions on the economy. The unions in the next two or three years, therefore, will devote more attention to discussing alternative policies with their own membership and beyond them the wider electorate.

Political objectives   Preparation for this campaign has given the union movement an opportunity to restate its political objectives, assess the worth of new policies and examine ways in which these could be achieved. A recent report on the organization and structure of the TUC marked the beginning of this process. The report has this to say about political objectives:

The fundamental objectives of the wider trade union movement, for example, full employment, economic growth, job and income security and improved social welfare, have not changed. These cannot be achieved without Government action.

'The Organization, Structure and Services of the TUC', December 1980.

You will recognize these objectives from Chapter three; they have not altered since 1945.

The alternative voice   While the objectives of unions have remained the same, the problems they face haven't. We have already seen how the depth of the recession, unemployment and the decline in membership have affected the unions. Their immediate response has been to campaign for alternative economic policies through the TUC and Labour Party. The unions, as before, are using the industrial and political wings of the movement to formulate and coordinate common policies to defend their interests in an uncertain economic climate. The recent TUC/Labour Party document, 'Economic Issues facing the next Labour Government' is a further step in this direction. Now, however, they have to go a stage further in ensuring that their policies find acceptance among the mass of working people.

The TUC is playing a central role in this attempt to get the arguments behind the alternative strategy to a wider audience. Here, membership education is seen as a means of countering much of the adverse publicity given to the unions in the press.

The Labour Party is also beginning to consider the need for a programme of political education in the run-up to the next election. Both these developments will focus on the campaign against unemployment and the present Government's economic policy. These issues, above all others, will restore the Labour Party's lost unity and give them and the unions some welcome political leverage.

The future of trade union power

It would be wrong, however, to assume that the return of a broad political consensus within the labour movement will automatically reverse the setbacks of the eighties. Our generation of workers, in keeping with previous generations, has encountered tremendous resistance to their attempts to both create and control change. Since 1945, we have seen the State adopting a strategy of cutting employment and setting limits to living standards while attempting to affect industrial reorganization and increase labour productivity. In the absence of effective sanctions our unions have found bargaining with governments more difficult than bargaining with the employer.

We've seen that during the first part of our period workers' control of the job has grown but trade union influence over the economy has lagged behind. But the current recession has even brought about a decline in workplace control and that has important implications for the future of our unions. If that decline is to be halted, and it is in our interest to see that it is, unions will have to look once again at the basics. The lessons we have learnt since the war tell us that unions can only progress by building on workplace solidarity.

Key points

● Unions in the '80s face a series of attacks from the Government, including restrictive legislation, the use of unemployment to weaken them and cuts in the public sector.

- Rapidly changing technology (especially micro-electronics) and the growth of massive multinational corporations present a long term challenge to the way trade unions operate.
- One result of these pressures is a fall in union membership.
- Unions are responding to this by recruitment campaigns and by considering mergers with other unions.
- The power of trade unionists at the workplace has also been challenged, with stewards and members being placed firmly on the defensive.
- There are signs that, in defending themselves, some of the old divisions in union ranks, like the one between 'staff' and 'manual' workers, are beginning to break down.
- Nationally trade union political objectives remain the same.
- A stronger TUC with more effective coordination and propaganda and a stronger union voice in the Labour Party are two ways in which trade unions have responded.
- The basis of strong trade unionism remains in the workplace, however and it is here that most of the hopes for changes in the '80s will rest.

Discussion

- How do you think union organization at your workplace will respond to the challenge of the '80s?
- What is the biggest problem facing organized workers today?
- What policies do you think unions should be arguing for?

Further reading

Some of the suggestions made elsewhere in the book, especially material on unemployment, are also relevant here. New technology is an area where there are some interesting union reports for example APEX's, 'Automation and the Office Worker' and the TUC's policy statement, 'Employment and

Technology'. There is an interesting discussion of some of the implications of current changes for trade union organization at a national level in a TUC consultative document, 'The organization, structure and services of the TUC'.

Workers' Report on Vickers by H. Beynon and H. Wainwright (Pluto Press), is a stimulating and recent account of the problems of organizing in a multinational company.

Material on new labour legislation comes out quite frequently. Just out as we write is *Employment Law under the Tories* from Pluto Press.

Finally if you've enjoyed reading this, you might consider reading other books covering a similar period. One suggestion is G. Goodman's, *The Awkward Warrior* which is a biography of the former TGWU general secretary, Frank Cousins. It is rather expensive but could be borrowed from the library.

Index

UNIONS AND CHANGE

growth 84, 85
importance of 43
public sector 14, 25, 42, 43, 44, 45, 46,
  47, 50, 77, 78, 81, 84, 88, 89, 90, 99,
  103
  attitudes towards 43
  employment 14, 25, 42, 43, 47, 48, 58,
    103, 133, 141, 175
  growth 84
  militancy 43, 89, 90, 108
  union membership 25, 27, 44, 45, 46,
    47, 48, 88, 89, 90, 183

railways 16, 18, 19, 20, 21, 25, 46, 120,
  130
rate for the job 32, 50, 74, 76
redundancy 24, 58, 97, 99, 100, 112, 114,
  115, 116, 117, 118, 119, 120, 121, 122,
  123, 124, 125, 126, 129, 139, 141, 142,
  143, 175, 181, 182, 183
  in cotton industry 18, 19, 20, 25, 115,
    116, 121, 122, 142
  effects of 58
  in motor industry 117, 118, 119
  on railways 121, 122
  strikes against 118, 119, 137, 138
  state policy 120, 121, 142
  union opposition to 116, 121, 122, 125,
    128, 136, 137, 141, 142, 143
  voluntary 127
Redundancy Payments Act, 1965 63,
  120, 121, 122, 123, 124, 125, 128, 129,
  136, 143
restrictive practices 113, 142
restructuring 131, 143
Robens Report 153, 154, 158, 161, 166

safety committees 152, 160, 165
safety policies 12, 46, 146, 151, 165
safety representatives 37, 146, 155, 157,
  159–61, 162, 163, 164, 165, 166, 167,
  168, 169, 170, 181, 182
  1978 regulations 159–61, 162, 167, 169
Scanlon, Hugh 40
self-employed 102
service industry 132, 133, 155, 175
shipbuilding 23, 32, 33, 61, 131, 138,
  139, 163
shop-stewards 17, 29, 30, 32, 34, 35, 36,
  37, 38, 39, 40, 41, 46, 50, 86, 96, 118,
  125, 128, 139, 149, 152, 162, 163, 181
  public sector 42, 46
  views on 38
  white collar 42
  workplace organization 11, 15, 26, 27,
    28, 29, 30, 31, 32, 33, 34, 36, 37, 39,
    40, 41, 42, 45, 49, 50, 86, 87, 113, 135,
    161, 171, 181
Social Contract 57, 102, 160

social services 55
social wage 101, 104, 105, 106, 141
  definition of 104, 105
  expanding 106, 141
  unions and 106
standard of living 12, 17, 24, 27, 52, 55,
  58, 69–112, 129, 133, 174, 176, 182
  economic growth and 17, 55, 82, 84
  measuring 70, 72, 73, 74, 76, 81
  pay 24, 70–73, 76, 88
  union control of 12, 27, 52, 71, 76, 82,
    84, 85, 87, 88, 89, 90, 145
  workers definition of 70, 71
state
  as employer 14, 25, 42, 43, 44, 45, 46,
    47, 58, 60, 67, 78, 100, 120, 133, 134,
    142
  intervention 100, 101, 109, 141
  standard of living 58, 77, 78, 100, 101,
    103, 104, 105, 106
  union relationship with 14, 17, 42, 43,
    46, 47, 51–67, 133, 140, 172
steel industry 13, 98, 143, 175, 182
strike(s) 17, 24, 25, 33, 34, 35, 38, 41, 46,
  47, 53, 54, 56, 62, 63, 87, 107, 108, 113,
  118, 119, 121, 124, 129, 137, 139, 140,
  142, 143, 158, 174, 182
  redundancy 118, 119, 123, 124, 137, 138
  seamen's 56
  supplementary benefit and 175
  wages 17, 24, 25, 41, 46, 47, 87, 107,
    108, 140, 174
  see also disputes

Taff Vale court case 53
tax changes 103, 105
textile workers 16, 18, 130, 131, 177
  see also cotton industry
Thatcher, Margaret 173, 176, 184
tinnitis 164
trade unions
  attacks on 173, 185
  changes in 11, 12, 45, 46, 47, 48, 49,
    52, 66, 140
  changes made by 12, 108, 143
  control 181
  density 15, 16, 17
  economic objectives 52, 66, 67, 102
  education 43, 52, 166
  growth 16, 23, 24, 42, 45, 50, 172, 176
  membership 11–27, 45, 50, 51, 133, 171,
    173, 176, 184, 186
  mergers 180, 181, 186
  militancy 24, 25, 43, 46, 63, 87, 117
  organization 11, 14, 15, 17, 22, 27
  political objectives 11, 58, 176, 184, 186
  power 17, 33, 52, 172, 183, 185
  representation 29–49, 63, 64, 116
  social objectives 12, 44, 52, 66, 67, 102